GREAT TASTES

COMFORT FOOD

First published in 2010 by Bay Books, an imprint of Murdoch Books Pty Limited
This edition published in 2010.

Murdoch Books Australia
Pier 8/9
23 Hickson Road
Millers Point NSW 2000
Phone: +61 (0) 2 8220 2000
Fax: +61 (0) 2 8220 2558
www.murdochbooks.com.au

Murdoch Books UK Limited
Erico House, 6th Floor
93–99 Upper Richmond Road
Putney, London SW15 2TG
Phone: +44 (0) 20 8785 5995
Fax: +44 (0) 20 8785 5985
www.murdochbooks.co.uk

Chief Executive: Juliet Rogers
Publishing Director: Kay Scarlett
Publisher: Lynn Lewis
Senior Designer: Heather Menzies
Designer: Craig Peterson
Production: Kita George
Index: Jo Rudd

ISBN: 9780681690868

PRINTED IN CHINA

OVEN GUIDE: You may find cooking times vary depending on the oven you are using. For fan-forced ovens, as a general rule, set the oven
temperature to 20°C (35°F) lower than indicated in the recipe.

GREAT TASTES

COMFORT FOOD

More than 120 easy recipes for every day

bay books

CONTENTS

COMFORT FOOD BASICS

Comfort food is a term that most of us use when we think of meals grandma used to make...those lovely robust roasts and delicious cakes and puddings, in particular, that aren't overly fancy or complicated but which deliver great flavour and make you feel good before, during and after you've eaten them! Comfort food is at the heart of family meals, relaxed get-togethers and winter warm-ups. It's good, honest food that takes you from breakfast to bedtime and leaves you sustained in mind, body and spirit.

The 'secret' behind cooking great comfort food is the same for all good cooking: Buy the best ingredients you can afford; make the most of seasonal produce; keep it simple, and keep a well-stocked pantry.

We employ some basic commonsense rules in the recipes in this book, to keep things simple. If the recipe doesn't state to 'cover' the pan or dish, then the food should be cooked uncovered. Also, we assume basic preparation of ingredients, such as washing and peeling of vegetables such as potatoes and onions—the recipe will, however, state if something is to be left unpeeled. .

Your Store cupboard

Although it is best to shop regularly for meat, seafood and seasonal vegetables and herbs, there are certain products that you will want to keep permanently in your storecupboard, to provide the backbone of your daily cooking. As a general rule, you should try to have in your pantry:

Baking powder

Beans, canned and dried

Breadcrumbs, dry and fresh (store the latter in the refrigerator)

Capers and other pickles

Cocoa powder

Coconut milk and coconut cream

Couscous

Dried fruits, such as raisins, currants, apricots

Flour (plain and self-raising) and cornflour

Gelatine

Honey

Mustards

Noodles

Nuts

Oils (olive, sesame, vegetable)

Olives

Pasta

Polenta

Rice, long-grain, short-grain and Arborio

Soy sauce and other Asian condiments

Stocks

Sugars

Tabasco

Tomatoes, canned

Tomato paste

Vinegars, white wine, red wine, brown and balsamic

Worcestershire sauce

Yeast, dried

These are all best stored in a cool, dark dry pantry. It is best to buy whole spices and grind them yourself, as needed—they stay fresher than the jars. However, if you prefer to buy jars of ready-ground spices and dried herbs, check them regularly for their aroma and appearance. Even though the use-by date may suggest that they are still in good condition, the colour and fragrance of them are better indicators.

Make sure bottles of oil are kept out of direct light, as they can become rancid. Should you choose to keep them in the fridge, the oil will thicken and appear cloudy—however, it will return to normal once it has reached room temperature again. Most bottles of sauces and condiments should be refrigerated once opened.

Keep potatoes and onions in a cool, dark place—though they must have adequate ventilation. Tomatoes, like most fruit, are best kept at room temperature, unless the weather is very hot or they are very ripe.

Your Fridge

Your fridge is somewhere where important hygiene rules come into play. When you get home with your shopping, unwrap meat or chicken and place on a plate large enough to prevent drips falling onto other food. Cover loosely with foil or plastic wrap.

Store vegetables unwashed (unless they are dried thoroughly, the moisture contributes to deterioration) in the crisper.

Many recipes will instruct you to cook something, then 'cool and refrigerate'. When you are doing this, cool the food as quickly as possible before refrigerating. Transfer it from the cooking pan to a wide bowl and stir frequently to release the heat. It is not necessary for the food to be completely cold prior to refrigerating it, just cooled. Don't put hot food in the fridge or freezer or it will raise the temperature inside, putting other foods at risk of deterioration.

The remaining contents of half-used cans should be put in a bowl or plastic container and refrigerated. Use them up within 2–3 days or discard them.

Thaw frozen food in the fridge, not at room temperature and never in a sink full of water. If you haven't removed food from the freezer in enough time, thaw it in the microwave.

Never refreeze thawed food. (Of course, you can thaw something, cook it and then freeze again—for instance frozen chicken that you might casserole and then freeze.)

Clean out your fridge, freezer and storecupboard regularly and remember—if you ever have even the slightest doubt about the freshness of a product, throw it out.

Cookery Terms

If there are any terms which aren't familiar to you in the recipes, you should find them here.

Al dente Italian phrase meaning 'to the tooth'. Refers to pasta and sometimes vegetables. Means slightly underdone, so still with some 'bite'.

Bain-marie Also called a 'water bath'. Usually a baking dish half-filled with water so delicate food is protected from direct heat. Often used for custards.

Bake blind To bake an empty pastry case before the filling is added. Ensures the pastry is cooked through and not soggy. Usually lined with baking paper and baking beads or rice or beans so it keeps its shape.

Baste To spoon or brush cooking juices or other fat over food during cooking.

Boil To cook liquid, or food in liquid, at 100°C (212°F). Large bubbles will break on the surface.

Bouquet garni A small bunch of fresh herbs used to flavour stocks, soups and stews. Removed before serving.

Brown To fry food (usually meat) quickly so that the outside is cooked and changes colour and juices are sealed in the meat.

Cube To chop food into even cubes. Usually bite-sized and for use in soups or stews so the size is not overly important. Dice are even smaller cubes.

Drain To remove liquid from food (usually with a colander or sieve). The food is kept and the liquid discarded unless specified.

En croûte Cooked entirely encased in pastry.

Escalope Very thin slice of meat, such as veal or chicken.

Flambé To pour liqueur over food (usually in the pan, over heat) and set fire to it.

Fold To mix one ingredient into another very gently (usually flour or egg whites) with a metal spoon or plastic spatula. The idea is to combine the mixture without losing the air. To fold properly, cut through the centre of the mixture, then run the edge of the spoon or spatula around the outer edge of the bowl, turning the bowl as you go.

Glaze A substance (often warmed jam or beaten egg) brushed over food to give it shine and colour.

Grease To lightly coat a tin or dish with oil or melted butter to prevent food sticking.

Infuse To flavour a liquid by heating it with aromatic ingredients (often spices) and leaving it to let the flavour develop.

Julienne To cut into uniform thin matchsticks for quick cooking. Often used for stir-fries or in French cuisine.

Knead To stretch and fold dough to make it firm and smooth. This stretches the gluten in the flour and gives elasticity. Used for bread making but not for pastry making (over-handling will make pastry tough).

Marinate To tenderize and flavour food (usually meat) by leaving it in an acidulated seasoned liquid (a marinade).

Parboil To partially cook in boiling water before some other form of cooking. Most commonly used for roast potatoes which are parboiled before being added to the roasting meat.

Poach To cook food immersed in a gently simmering liquid.

Punch down the dough A term used in bread making. A yeast dough which is left to rise is then punched with one firm blow of the fist, to remove the air from it.

Purée Food blended or processed to a pulp.

Reduce To boil or simmer liquid in an uncovered pan so that the liquid evaporates and the mixture becomes thicker and more concentrated in flavour. Most soups and stews are reduced—this should usually be done at a simmer so that the flavour of the dish is not impaired by long, hard boiling.

Roux The basic mixture of many sauces—fat (usually melted butter) and flour. Used to thicken. Liquid is added for a sauce.

Rub in To combine flour and butter with your fingertips, usually for pastry. It will resemble fine breadcrumbs.

Score To ensure even cooking. Make incisions with a knife (usually into fish or meat), but do not cut all the way through.

Simmer To cook liquid, or food in liquid, over low heat, below boiling point. The surface of the liquid will be moving with a few small bubbles.

Skim To remove fat that comes to the surface of a liquid.

Stir-fry To quickly fry (in a wok) over high heat while stirring.

Strain To remove solids from a liquid by pouring through a sieve. The solids are discarded, unless specified.

Whisk To beat rapidly with a wire whisk, to incorporate air and add volume.

Zest The coloured skin of citrus fruits. Avoid the bitter white pith that is below it.

BREAKFAST

EGGS BENEDICT

SERVES 4

12 eggs, straight from the fridge

8 slices prosciutto

4 English muffins, split

200 g (7 oz) butter

2 tablespoons lemon juice

1 **Turn on the grill (broiler)**. Put a large frying pan full of water over high heat. When the water is bubbling, turn the heat down to a simmer. Crack an egg into a cup and slip the egg into the water. The egg should start to turn opaque as it hits the water. Do the same with 7 more eggs, keeping them separated. Turn heat down and leave the eggs for 3 minutes.

2 **Put the prosciutto** on a baking tray, place it under the grill for 2 minutes; turn it over and cook the other side. Put muffins in a toaster or under the grill to toast.

3 **Crack the remaining** 4 eggs into a blender, put the lid on and leave the top hole open. Heat the butter in a small pan, until it has melted.

4 **Start the blender** and pour in the butter in a steady stream through the top hole. The eggs should thicken straight away to make a thick hollandaise sauce. Add the lemon juice and season the hollandaise with salt and black pepper.

5 **Put the muffins** on plates and put a slice of prosciutto on each. Lift each egg out of the water, drain and put them on top of the prosciutto. Spoon some hollandaise over each egg.

FRENCH TOAST WITH CRISPY PROSCIUTTO

SERVES 4

3 tablespoons thick (double/heavy) cream
3 eggs
3 tablespoons caster (superfine) sugar
pinch of cinnamon
8 thick slices bread, cut in half diagonally
about 80 g (3 oz/⅓ cup) butter
1 tablespoon olive oil
12 slices prosciutto

1   Put the cream, eggs, sugar and cinnamon in a wide, shallow bowl and mix together. Soak the bread in the egg mixture, one slice at a time, shaking off any excess.

2   Melt half the butter in a frying pan. When it is sizzling, add 3–4 slices of bread in a single layer and cook until golden brown on both sides. Cook the remaining bread in batches, adding more butter as needed, and keeping the cooked slices warm in the oven until all are done.

3   Next, in a separate frying pan, heat the olive oil. When hot, add the prosciutto and fry until crisp. Remove and drain on paper towels. Place the prosciutto on top of the French toast and serve.

EGGS AND TOMATOES ON SPRING ONION POTATO CAKES

SERVES 2

SPRING ONION POTATO CAKES

300 g (11 oz) potatoes, roughly chopped

1 egg yolk

50 g (2 oz) grated cheddar cheese

3 spring onions (scallions), finely
  chopped

2 tablespoons finely chopped flat-leaf
  (Italian) parsley

1 tablespoon plain (all-purpose) flour

2 tablespoons olive oil

4 tablespoons olive oil

1 garlic clove, sliced

3 roma (plum) tomatoes, halved
  lengthways

butter, for frying

4 eggs

1 Boil the potato in a saucepan of salted water until tender. Drain, then return potato to the pan over low heat to allow any moisture to evaporate. Remove the pan from the heat and mash the potato. Stir in the egg yolk, cheese, spring onion and parsley and season. Form into four patty shapes. Tip the flour onto a plate and lightly coat the patties with it. Cover and chill for 30 minutes.

2 Heat the olive oil in a large frying pan over medium heat. Fry the patties for 4–5 minutes on both sides until golden brown. Keep warm until needed.

3 In a separate frying pan, heat 2 tablespoons of the olive oil in the pan over low heat. Add garlic and fry for 2 minutes. Add the tomatoes, cut side down, and fry for 10–15 minutes, turning them once during cooking.

4 Meanwhile, heat a heavy-based non-stick frying pan over medium heat and add the remaining oil and a little butter. When the butter is sizzling, break the eggs into the frying pan and fry. Cook for about 1 minute. Turn off the heat and leave to stand for 1 minute. Serve the eggs with the spring onion potato cakes and tomatoes.

SERVES 4

2 tablespoons olive oil

1 large onion, thinly sliced

2 red capsicums (peppers), seeded and membrane removed, cut into thin strips

2 garlic cloves, crushed

750 g (1 lb 10 oz) tomatoes

pinch of cayenne pepper

8 eggs, lightly beaten

1 tablespoon butter

4 thin slices good-quality ham

1 Heat the oil in a large, heavy-based frying pan over medium heat, then add the onion. Cook for about 3 minutes, or until soft. Add the capsicum and garlic, cover and cook for 8 minutes, stirring frequently to ensure the mixture doesn't brown.

2 Score a cross in the base of each tomato. Put in a large bowl of boiling water for 30 seconds, then drain and plunge into a bowl of cold water. Remove the tomatoes and peel the skin away from the cross. Chop the flesh and discard the cores. Add the chopped tomato and cayenne to the capsicum mixture, cover the pan and cook for a further 5 minutes.

3 Uncover the pan and increase the heat. Cook 3 minutes, or until the juices have evaporated, shaking the pan often. Season well with salt and freshly ground black pepper.

4 Add eggs and scramble into the mixture until fully cooked.

5 Heat the butter in a small frying pan over medium heat and fry the ham. Arrange the piperade on four plates, top with the cooked ham and serve with buttered toast.

SCRAMBLED EGGS AND SALMON ON BRIOCHE

SERVES 2

4 fresh eggs

4 tablespoons cream

2 tablespoons unsalted butter

125 g (4½ oz) smoked salmon, sliced

2 teaspoons finely chopped dill

2 individual brioche buns or 2 croissants

1 **Crack the eggs** into a bowl, add the cream and beat well together. Season with salt and freshly ground black pepper.

2 **Melt the butter** in a non-stick frying pan. When it starts to sizzle, add the eggs and turn the heat down to low. Using a flat-ended wooden spoon, push the mixture around until it starts to set, then add the salmon and dill. Continue to cook, gently folding the salmon and dill through the mixture until the eggs are mostly cooked, and just a little liquid left in the pan.

3 **Cut the top off** the brioche or croissants, scoop out some of the filling, then pile the scrambled eggs on top and serve.

CROQUE MADAME

MAKES 2

3 eggs

1 tablespoon milk

1½ tablespoons butter, softened

4 slices good-quality white bread

1 teaspoon dijon mustard

4 slices gruyère cheese

2 slices leg ham

2 teaspoons oil

1 Crack 1 egg into a wide, shallow bowl, add the milk and lightly beat. Season with salt and freshly ground black pepper.

2 Butter the bread using ½ tablespoon of butter and spread half the slices with dijon mustard. Place a slice of cheese on top, then the ham and then another slice of cheese. Top with the remaining bread.

3 Heat the remaining butter and oil in a large non-stick frying pan over medium heat. While the butter is melting, dip one sandwich into the egg and milk mixture, coating the bread on both sides. When the butter is sizzling but not brown, add the sandwich and cook for 1½ minutes on one side, pressing down firmly with a spatula. Turn over and cook the other side, then move it to the side of the pan.

4 Gently break an egg into the pan and fry until it is done to your liking.

5 Transfer the sandwich to a plate and top with the fried egg. Keep warm while you repeat with the remaining sandwich and egg, adding more butter and oil to the pan if necessary. Serve immediately.

FRIED EGG AND RED ONION WRAP

SERVES 4

1½ tablespoons olive oil

3 red onions, thickly sliced

1 large red capsicum (pepper), seeded and membrane removed, sliced

3 tablespoons balsamic vinegar

4 eggs

4 lavash breads

4 tablespoons sour cream

sweet chilli sauce, to drizzle

1 Heat the olive oil in a non-stick frying pan and add the onion. Cook it slowly, stirring occasionally until it softens and turns translucent. Add the red capsicum and continue cooking until both the onion and capsicum are soft. Turn the heat up and stir for a minute or two, or until they start to brown, then stir in the balsamic vinegar. Remove the mixture from the pan and keep warm.

2 Carefully break the eggs into the frying pan, keeping them separate if you can. Cook over a gentle heat until the eggs are just set.

3 Heat the lavash breads in a microwave or under a grill (broiler) for a few seconds (you want them to be soft and warm). Lay the breads out on a board, spread a tablespoon of sour cream onto the centre of each, then drizzle with a little chilli sauce. Put a heap of the onion and capsicum mixture on each and top with an egg. Season with salt and pepper.

4 Fold in one short end of each piece of lavash bread and then roll each one up lengthways.

GRILLED FIELD MUSHROOMS WITH CHILLI

SERVES 4

4 large or 8 medium field mushrooms

2 tablespoons butter, softened

1 garlic clove, crushed

1–2 small red chillies, finely chopped

4 tablespoons finely chopped parsley

4 thick slices ciabatta

tomato chutney or relish

crème fraîche or sour cream, to serve

1 Put the grill (broiler) on and cover the grill rack with a piece of foil so any juices stay with the mushrooms as they cook. Gently pull the stalks out of the mushrooms and peel off the skins.

2 Combine the butter, garlic, chilli and parsley and spread some over the inside of each mushroom. Make sure the butter is quite soft so it spreads easily. Season well.

3 Grill the mushrooms under medium heat for about 8 minutes—they need to be cooked right through. Test the centres with the point of a knife if you are not sure.

4 Toast the bread, spread tomato chutney or relish on each slice, then top with a mushroom (or two). Serve with a dollop of crème fraîche or sour cream.

SAVOURY BREAKFAST TARTS

SERVES 4

220 g (8 oz/1½ cups) plain (all-purpose)
    flour

½ teaspoon salt

140 g (5 oz) butter, diced

4 slices ham

2 tablespoons chopped parsley

2 medium tomatoes, finely chopped

9 eggs

125 ml (4 fl oz/½ cup) cream

4 tablespoons grated parmesan cheese

1 **Preheat the oven** to 200°C (400°F/Gas 6). Sift the flour and salt into a food processor, add the butter and process for a few seconds until the mixture resembles breadcrumbs. Bring the dough together using your hands and shape into a ball. Wrap the ball in plastic wrap, flatten slightly, and put in the fridge for 10 minutes.

2 **Roll the pastry** out on a floured work surface until it is very thin. Cut out four 16 cm (6½ inch) circles and use them to line four 10 cm (4 inch) tartlet tins. Press the pastry gently into the flutes of the tins. Line each tin with a piece of crumpled baking paper and some uncooked rice. Bake the pastry for 5 minutes, then take out the paper and rice and bake for another minute.

3 **Line each pastry** base with the ham (you may need to cut it into pieces to make it fit neatly). Sprinkle with the parsley and add the tomato. Gently break two eggs into each tin, then pour a quarter of the cream over the top of each, sprinkle with parmesan cheese and dust with salt and pepper.

4 **Put the tarts** in the oven and bake for 10–12 minutes, or until the egg whites are set. Serve hot or cold.

CHEESE CORNBREAD WITH SCRAMBLED EGGS

SERVES 4

CHEESE CORNBREAD

155 g (5½ oz/1 cup) self-raising flour

1 tablespoon caster (superfine) sugar

2 teaspoons baking powder

1 teaspoon salt

110 g (4 oz/¾ cup) fine polenta

60 g (2 oz/½ cup) grated cheddar cheese

30 g (1 oz/½ cup) fresh chopped mixed herbs (chives, dill, parsley)

2 eggs

250 ml (9 fl oz/1 cup) buttermilk

4 tablespoons macadamia or olive oil

SCRAMBLED EGGS

6 eggs

125 ml (4 fl oz/½ cup) pouring cream

small basil leaves, to garnish

1 Preheat oven to 180°C (350°F/Gas 4) and grease a 20 cm x 10 cm (8 x 4 inch) loaf (bar) tin. Sift flour, sugar, baking powder and salt into a bowl. Add the polenta, cheddar, herbs, eggs, buttermilk and oil and mix to combine. Spoon mixture into the loaf tin and bake for 45 minutes, or until a skewer inserted into the centre comes out clean. Remove from the tin.

2 To make the scrambled eggs, whisk together the eggs and cream and season with salt and pepper. Pour mixture into a non-stick frying pan and cook over low heat, stirring occasionally until the egg is just set. (The more you stir the eggs, the more scrambled they become.) Serve scrambled eggs with slices of buttered cornbread. Sprinkle with basil.

HUEVOS RANCHEROS

SERVES 4

1½ tablespoons olive oil

1 white onion, finely chopped

1 green capsicum (pepper), seeded and membrane removed, finely chopped

2 red chillies, finely chopped

1 garlic clove, crushed

½ teaspoon dried oregano

2 tomatoes, chopped

2 x 400 g (14 oz) tin chopped tomatoes

8 eggs

4 flour tortillas

100 g (3½ oz/⅔ cup) feta cheese, crumbled

1 **Put the olive oil** in a large frying pan (one with a lid) over medium heat. Add the onion and green capsicum and fry them gently together for 3 minutes, or until they are soft.

2 **Add chilli and garlic** and stir briefly, then add the oregano, fresh and tinned tomatoes, and 185 ml (6 fl oz./¾ cup) water. Bring to the boil, then turn down the heat, cover with a lid and simmer gently for 8–10 minutes, or until the sauce thickens. Season with salt and pepper.

3 **Smooth the surface** of the mixture. Make eight hollows with the back of a spoon. Break an egg into each hollow and put the lid on the pan. Cook the eggs for 5 minutes, or until they are set.

4 **While the eggs** are cooking, heat the tortillas according to the instructions on the packet and cut each into quarters.

5 **Serve the eggs** with some feta crumbled over them and the tortillas on the side.

MUSHROOM OMELETTE WITH CHORIZO

SERVES 2

50 g (2 oz) butter

1 chorizo sausage, sliced

100 g (3½ oz) mushrooms, finely sliced

6 eggs

2 tablespoons finely chopped chives

1 Beat 30 g (1 oz) of butter in a small omelette pan or frying pan over medium heat. Add the chorizo and fry for about 5 minutes, or until golden. Remove from pan using a slotted spoon. Add the mushrooms to the pan and cook, stirring frequently, for about 4 minutes, or until soft. Add to the chorizo.

2 Break the eggs into a bowl and season with salt and freshly ground black pepper. Add the chives and beat lightly with a fork.

3 Put half the remaining butter in the pan and melt over medium heat until foaming. Add half the eggs and cook for 20 seconds, in which time they will start to set on the bottom, then quickly stir the mixture with a fork. Work quickly, drawing away some of the cooked egg from the bottom of the pan and allowing some of the uncooked egg to set, tilting the pan a little as you go. Once the eggs are mostly set, arrange half the mushrooms and chorizo on top. Cook for 1 minute more, if necessary. Tip the omelette out onto a plate and keep warm while the second omelette is cooking. Repeat with the remaining ingredients. Serve as soon as both omelettes are cooked.

BANANA BREAD

MAKES 1 LOAF

3 ripe bananas, well mashed

2 eggs, well beaten

2 teaspoons grated orange zest

250 g (9 oz/1⅔ cups) plain (all-purpose) flour

1 teaspoon ground cinnamon

1 teaspoon salt

1 teaspoon bicarbonate of soda (baking soda)

175 g (6 oz/¾ cup) caster (superfine) sugar

75 g (2½ oz/2 cups) walnuts, coarsely chopped

1   Preheat oven to 180°C (350°F/Gas 4). Grease a 17 x 8 cm (7 x 3 inch) loaf (bar) tin.

2   Combine the bananas, eggs and orange zest in a large bowl. Sift in the flour, cinnamon, salt and bicarbonate of soda, mix, then add the sugar and walnuts. Mix thoroughly, then tip into the prepared tin. Bake for 1 hour 10 minutes, or until a skewer inserted into the centre comes out clean.

3   To serve, eat warm or allow to cool, then toast and serve buttered.

MAKES 960 G (2 LB 2 OZ/8 CUPS)
DRY WEIGHT

400 g (14 oz/4 cups) rolled (porridge) oats
100 g (3½ oz/1 cup) rice flakes
125 g (4½ oz/1 cup) barley flakes
125 g (4½ oz/1 cup) rye flakes
200 g (7 oz/1 cup) millet

1 Put all the ingredients in a large bowl and stir together thoroughly. Store dry porridge mixture in an airtight container until ready to use.

2 To prepare porridge for four people, put 280 g (10 oz/ 2 cups) of the dry porridge mix in a saucepan with a pinch of sea salt and 500 ml (17 fl oz/2 cups) water. Stir well and leave to stand for about 5 minutes (this creates a smoother, creamier porridge).

3 Stir the porridge a few times, then pour in another 500 ml (17 fl oz/2 cups) water. Bring to the boil over medium heat, stirring occasionally. Reduce the heat to low and simmer, stirring often, for 12–15 minutes, or until the porridge is soft and creamy and the grains are cooked.

Note: This porridge is delicious served with your choice of milk, a dollop of yoghurt, a drizzle of honey, golden syrup or maple syrup, or a sprinkling of dark brown sugar.

BLUEBERRY PANCAKES

MAKES ABOUT 12 PANCAKES

250 ml (9 fl oz/1 cup) buttermilk

1 egg, lightly beaten

1 tablespoon melted butter

1 teaspoon natural vanilla extract

115 g (4 oz/¾ cup) plain (all-purpose) flour

1 teaspoon baking powder

½ teaspoon salt

2 ripe bananas, mashed

100 g (3½ oz/⅔ cup) blueberries

1 teaspoon oil

maple syrup, to serve

1   Put the buttermilk, egg, butter and vanilla extract in a bowl and whisk together. Sift in the flour, baking powder and salt, then stir, making sure not to over blend as the batter should be lumpy. Add the fruit.

2   Heat the oil in a frying pan over medium heat. Add 3 tablespoons of batter to the pan for each pancake. Cook for 3 minutes, or until the pancakes are golden brown on the bottom. Turn over and cook for 1 minute more. Repeat with the rest of the batter, keeping the cooked pancakes warm. Serve immediately, drizzled with maple syrup.

GINGER AND RICOTTA FLATCAKES WITH HONEYCOMB

SERVES 4

150 g (5½ oz/1 cup) wholemeal (whole-wheat) flour

2 teaspoons baking powder

2 teaspoons ground ginger

2 tablespoons caster (superfine) sugar

55 g (2 oz/1 cup) flaked coconut, toasted

4 eggs, separated

500 g (1 lb 2 oz/2 cups) ricotta cheese

310 ml (11 fl oz/1¼ cups) milk

4 bananas, sliced

200 g (7 oz) fresh honeycomb, broken into large pieces

1   Sift the flour, baking powder, ginger and sugar into a bowl. Stir in the coconut and make a well in the centre. Add the combined egg yolks, 350 g (12 oz) of the ricotta and all of the milk. Mix until smooth.

2   Beat the egg whites until soft peaks form, then fold into the pancake mixture.

3   Heat a frying pan over a low heat and brush lightly with a little melted butter or oil. Pour 3 tablespoons of the batter into the pan and swirl gently to create an even pancake. Cook until bubbles form on the surface. Flip and cook the other side for 1 minute, or until golden. Repeat until all the batter is used up.

4   Stack three pancakes onto each plate and top with a generous dollop of ricotta, banana and a large piece of fresh honeycomb.

GRILLED STONE FRUITS WITH CINNAMON TOAST

SERVES 4

2 tablespoons butter

1½ teaspoons ground cinnamon

4 thick slices good-quality brioche

4 ripe plums, halved and stones removed

4 ripe nectarines, halved and stones removed

2 tablespoons warmed blossom honey

1 Place the butter and 1 teaspoon of the ground cinnamon in a bowl and mix until well combined. Grill (broil) the brioche on one side until golden. Spread the other side with half the cinnamon butter, then grill until golden. Keep warm in the oven.

2 Brush the plums and nectarines with the remaining butter and cook under a grill (broiler) or on a ridged grill plate, until the spread is bubbling and the fruit is tinged at the edges.

3 To serve, place 2 plum halves and 2 nectarine halves on each toasted slice of brioche. Dust with the remaining cinnamon and drizzle with the warmed honey.

Note: Tinned plums or apricots may be used in place of fresh stone fruits.

CINNAMON PORRIDGE WITH FIGS AND CREAM

SERVES 4

200 g (7 oz/2 cups) rolled (porridge) oats
¼ teaspoon ground cinnamon
50 g (2 oz) butter
115 g (4 oz/½ cup) soft brown sugar
300 ml (10½ fl oz) cream
6 fresh figs, halved
milk, to serve
thick (double/heavy) cream, to serve

1 **Place the oats**, 1 litre (35 fl oz/4 cups) water and cinnamon in a saucepan. Stir over medium heat for 5 minutes, or until the porridge becomes thick and smooth. Set the porridge aside.

2 **Melt butter** in a large frying pan, add all but 2 tablespoons of the brown sugar and stir until it dissolves. Stir in the cream and bring to the boil, then simmer for 5 minutes, or until the sauce starts to thicken slightly.

3 **Place the figs** on a baking tray, sprinkle with the remaining sugar and grill (broil) until the sugar is melted.

4 **Spoon the porridge** into individual bowls, top with a little milk, then divide the figs and caramel sauce among the bowls. Top each serving with a large dollop of thick cream.

LUNCH

CORNISH PASTIES

MAKES 6

SHORTCRUST (PIE) PASTRY

310 g (11 oz/2 cups) plain (all-purpose) flour

125 g (4½ oz) chilled butter, cubed

80–100 ml (2½–3½ fl oz) iced water

165 g (6 oz) round steak, finely chopped

1 small potato, finely chopped

1 small onion, finely chopped

1 small carrot, finely chopped

1–2 teaspoons worcestershire sauce

2 tablespoons beef stock

1 egg, lightly beaten

1 **Lightly grease a baking tray**. Sift the flour and a pinch of salt into a large bowl. Using your fingertips, rub in the butter until the mixture resembles fine breadcrumbs. Make a well in the centre and add almost all the water. Mix together with a flat-bladed knife, using a cutting action, until the mixture comes together in beads. Add more water if the dough is too dry. Turn out onto a lightly floured work surface and form into a ball. Cover with plastic wrap and refrigerate for 20 minutes.

2 **Preheat the oven** to 210°C (415°F/Gas 6–7). Mix together the steak, potato, onion, carrot, worcestershire sauce and stock in a bowl and season well.

3 **Divide the dough** into six portions. Roll out each portion to 3 mm (⅛ in) thick. Using a 16 cm (6 inch) diameter plate as a guide, cut six circles. Divide the filling among the circles.

4 **Brush the edges** with beaten egg and bring the pastry together to form a semi-circle. Pinch the edges into a frill and place on the tray. Brush the pastry with beaten egg and bake for 15 minutes. Reduce the oven to 180°C (350°F/Gas 4) and cook for 25–30 minutes, or until golden.

POTATO PIES

MAKES 6

1 kg (2 lb 4 oz) all-purpose potatoes, chopped
1 tablespoon oil
1 onion, finely chopped
1 garlic clove, crushed
500 g (1 lb 2 oz) minced (ground) beef
2 tablespoons plain (all-purpose) flour
500 ml (17 fl oz/2 cups) beef stock
2 tablespoons tomato paste (concentrated purée)
1 tablespoon worcestershire sauce
500 g (1 lb 2 oz) ready-rolled shortcrust (pie) pastry
50 g (2 oz) butter, softened
3 tablespoons milk

1　Boil the potatoes for about 10 minutes, or until tender. Drain, then mash.

2　Preheat the oven to 210°C (415°F/Gas 6–7). Grease six 11 cm (4 inch) pie tins.

3　Heat the oil in a frying pan, add the onion and cook for 5 minutes, or until soft. Add the garlic and cook for 1 minute. Add the beef and cook over medium heat for 5 minutes, or until browned, breaking up any lumps with a fork.

4　Sprinkle the flour over the meat and stir to combine. Add the stock, tomato paste, worcestershire sauce and some salt and pepper to the pan and stir for 2 minutes. Bring to the boil, then reduce the heat slightly and simmer for 5 minutes, or until the mixture has reduced and thickened. Allow to cool completely before the next step.

5　Roll out the pastry between two sheets of baking paper and, using a plate as a guide, cut the pastry into 15 cm (6 inch) circles and line the pie tins. Cut baking paper to cover each tin, spread baking beads or uncooked rice over the paper and bake for 7 minutes. Remove the paper and beads and cook the pastry for a further 5 minutes. Cool.

6　Divide the meat filling among the pastry cases. Stir the butter and milk into the mashed potato and pipe or spread all over the top of the meat filling. Bake for 20 minutes, or until lightly golden.

SNAPPER PIES

SERVES 4

2 tablespoons olive oil

4 onions, thinly sliced

375 ml (13 fl oz/1½ cups) fish stock

875 ml (30 fl oz/3½ cups) cream

1 kg (2 lb 4 oz) skinless snapper fillets,
   cut into large pieces

2 sheets puff pastry, thawed

1 egg, lightly beaten

1 **Preheat the oven** to 220°C (425°F/Gas 7). Heat the oil in a deep frying pan, add the onion and stir over medium heat for 20 minutes, or until the onion is slightly caramelized. Add the fish stock, bring to the boil and cook for 10 minutes, or until the liquid is nearly evaporated. Stir in the cream and bring to the boil. Reduce the heat and simmer for 20 minutes, or until the liquid is reduced by half.

2 **Divide half the sauce** among four 500 ml (17 fl oz/2 cup) ramekins. Place some fish pieces in each ramekin and top with the remaining sauce. Cut the pastry sheets slightly larger than the tops of the ramekins. Brush the edges of the pastry with a little of the egg, press the pastry onto the ramekins and brush the pastry top with the remaining beaten egg. Bake for 30 minutes, or until well puffed.

CHICKEN AND LEEK PIES

SERVES 4

60 g (2¼ oz) butter

1 leek, white part only, thinly sliced

4 skinless, boneless chicken breasts (about 200 g/7 oz each), chopped into bite-sized pieces

50 g (2 oz) plain (all-purpose) flour

250 ml (9 fl oz/1 cup) chicken stock

300 ml (10½ fl oz) cream

155 g (5½ oz/1 cup) fresh or frozen peas, blanched

1 sheet puff pastry, thawed

1 Preheat oven to 200°C (400°F/Gas 6). Melt butter in a large saucepan over a medium heat and cook the leek for 2 minutes, or until soft. Add chicken and cook for 4–5 minutes, or until cooked. Add the flour and cook, stirring, until it starts to bubble. Add the stock and cook until the mixture starts to thicken. Add cream, reserving 1 tablespoon to glaze pastry. Cook until the mixture just starts to boil. Stir in the peas. Season. Remove from the heat.

2 Divide the filling among four individual pie dishes or ramekins. Top with a circle of pastry, cut just bigger than the top of the dish, then press around the edges to seal. Brush the surface with the cream. Make a slit in the top to allow steam to escape.

3 Place dishes on a metal tray and bake for 20–25 minutes, or until the pastry is golden.

TOASTED CHEESE, AÏOLI AND HAM SANDWICH

SERVES 4

1 loaf ciabatta, Turkish bread or soft
  white bread of your choice

1 garlic clove, crushed

125 g (4½ oz/½ cup) mayonnaise

4 slices ham

100 g (3½ oz) semi-dried (sun-blushed)
  tomatoes, chopped

2 tablespoons capers, chopped

6–8 slices cheddar cheese

1 **Turn on the grill (broiler)**. Cut bread in half horizontally and then into four equal pieces. Toast all the pieces. To make the aïoli, mix the garlic into the mayonnaise and season it well with salt and pepper.

2 **Spread aïoli** over the insides of each sandwich. Put a slice of ham on four of the pieces and then divide the semi-dried tomatoes and capers among them. Top with enough cheese slices to make a good layer. Put sandwiches on a baking tray.

3 **Grill the sandwiches** until the cheese melts and starts to bubble and then put the tops back on and press firmly.

4 **Cut each sandwich** in half diagonally and enjoy.

MEDITERRANEAN BLT

SERVES 4

4 small vine-ripened tomatoes, halved

1 head of garlic, halved

1 tablespoon extra virgin olive oil

3 tablespoons basil leaves

1 loaf Italian wood-fired bread

8 slices provolone cheese

8 slices mortadella

1 large handful rocket (arugula)

extra virgin olive oil, extra, to drizzle

balsamic vinegar, to drizzle

1   Preheat oven to 200°C (400°F/Gas 6). Place the tomato and garlic in a roasting tin and drizzle with the oil. Sprinkle with sea salt and cracked black pepper and roast for 40 minutes, or until the garlic is soft and the tomatoes are slightly dried. Add basil leaves and continue cooking for 5 minutes, or until the leaves are crisp. Remove from the oven.

2   Cut four thick slices from the loaf of wood-fired bread and lightly toast on both sides. Peel the roasted garlic cloves and spread half onto the toast. Top with the provolone, mortadella, rocket, basil and roasted tomatoes. Sprinkle with the remaining roasted garlic, drizzle with extra olive oil and the balsamic vinegar and serve immediately.

SPINACH AND ZUCCHINI FRITTATA

SERVES 4

1 tablespoon olive oil

1 red onion, thinly sliced

2 zucchini (courgettes), sliced

1 garlic clove, crushed

300 g (10½ oz) baby English spinach leaves, stalks removed

6 eggs

2 tablespoons cream

80 g (3 oz) Emmenthal cheese, grated

1 Heat the oil in a non-stick frying pan and fry the onion and zucchini over medium heat until they are a pale golden brown. Add the garlic and cook it for a minute. Add the spinach and cook until the spinach has wilted and any excess moisture has evaporated off—if you don't do this, your frittata will end up soggy in the middle, as the liquid will continue to come out as it cooks. Shake the pan so you get an even layer of mixture. Turn the heat down to low.

2 Beat the eggs and cream together and season with salt and pepper.

3 Stir in half of the cheese and pour the mixture over the spinach. Cook the bottom of the frittata for about 4 minutes, or until the egg is just set. While you are doing this, turn on the grill (broiler). When the bottom of the frittata is set, scatter on the rest of the cheese and put the frying pan under the grill to cook the top.

4 Turn the frittata out of the frying pan after leaving it to set for a minute. Cut it into wedges to serve.

MINESTRONE WITH PESTO

SERVES 4

1 tablespoon olive oil

1 small onion, finely chopped

1 garlic clove, finely chopped

1 tablespoon finely chopped parsley

55 g (2 oz) pancetta, cubed

1 celery stalk, halved, then sliced

1 carrot, sliced

1 teaspoon tomato paste (concentrated purée)

200 g (7 oz) tinned chopped tomatoes

1 litre (35 fl oz/4 cups) chicken or vegetable stock

1 zucchini (courgette), sliced

2 tablespoons peas

6 runner beans, cut into 2.5 cm (1 inch) lengths

1 handful shredded savoy cabbage

2 tablespoons ditalini

100 g (3½ oz) tinned borlotti (cranberry) beans, rinsed and drained

2 tablespoons ready-made pesto

1 Melt the oil in a large saucepan and add the onion, garlic, parsley and pancetta. Cook everything over very low heat, stirring the mixture once or twice, for about 10 minutes, or until the onion is soft and golden. If your heat won't go very low, keep an eye on everything and stir more often.

2 Add the celery and carrot and cook them for 5 minutes. Stir in the tomato paste and chopped tomato with plenty of pepper. Add the stock and bring slowly to the boil. Cover and leave to simmer for 30 minutes, stirring once or twice.

3 Taste the soup for seasoning, adjust if necessary, then add the zucchini, peas, runner beans, cabbage, ditalini and borlotti beans. Simmer everything for a couple of minutes until the pasta is just tender. Serve with some pesto spooned into the middle of each bowl of minestrone.

GRILLED NACHOS

SERVES 4

2 x 300 g (10½ oz) packets corn chips

4 tomatoes, chopped

1 red onion, finely chopped

3 jalapeño chillies, thinly sliced

2 tablespoons lime juice

4 tablespoons chopped coriander
(cilantro) leaves

220 g (8 oz/1½ cups) feta cheese,
crumbled

1 Turn on the grill (broiler). Arrange the corn chips on four ovenproof plates.

2 Scatter the tomato, onion and chilli on top of the corn chips, then drizzle with the lime juice and season with some salt. Scatter the coriander and feta cheese over the top, making sure the corn chips are well covered.

3 Grill (broil) the nachos until they start to brown around the edges and the cheese starts to melt. Serve hot but be careful of the plates—they will be very hot too.

CHILLI CON CARNE

SERVES 4

1 tablespoon oil

1 large red onion, finely chopped

2 garlic cloves, crushed

1½ teaspoons chilli powder

1 teaspoon ground oregano

2 teaspoons ground cumin

500 g (1 lb 2 oz) lean minced (ground) beef

2 x 400 g (14 oz) tins chopped tomatoes

420 g (15 oz) tin red kidney beans, rinsed and drained

8 flour tortillas

sour cream, to serve

1 **Preheat the oven** to 180°C (350°F/Gas 4). Heat the oil in a large saucepan, add the onion and garlic and cook, stirring, over medium heat for about 2–3 minutes, or until softened. Add the chilli powder, oregano and cumin and stir until fragrant. Add the beef and cook, stirring, for about 5 minutes, or until browned all over, breaking up any lumps with the back of a wooden spoon.

2 **Add the tomato**, beans and 125 ml (4 fl oz/½ cup) water and simmer, stirring occasionally, for about 30 minutes, or until thick. Season to taste with salt and pepper. About 10 minutes before serving, wrap the tortillas in foil and heat them in the oven according to packet instructions to soften. Fill the tortillas with the chilli and wrap. Serve with sour cream and, if desired, a green salad.

Note: You can top jacket potatoes with chilli con carne and a dollop of sour cream.

TURKISH PIZZA

MAKES 8

1 teaspoon dried yeast

½ teaspoon sugar

225 g (8 oz/1½ cups) plain (all-purpose) flour

1 teaspoon salt

4 tablespoons olive oil

250 g (9 oz) onions, finely chopped

500 g (1 lb 2 oz) minced (ground) lamb

2 garlic cloves

1 teaspoon ground cinnamon

1½ teaspoons ground cumin

½ teaspoon cayenne pepper

3 tablespoons tomato paste (concentrated purée)

400 g (14 oz) tin crushed tomatoes

4 tablespoons pine nuts

3 tablespoons chopped coriander (cilantro) leaves

Greek-style yoghurt, to serve

1 Mix the yeast, sugar and 60 ml (2 fl oz/¼ cup) warm water in a bowl. Leave in a warm, draught-free place for 10 minutes.

2 Sift the flour and salt into a large bowl, stir in the yeast mixture, 1 tablespoon of the oil and about 100 ml (3½ fl oz) warm water. Mix to form a soft dough, then turn onto a floured board and knead for 10 minutes, or until smooth. Place in an oiled bowl, cover and leave in a warm place for 1 hour.

3 Heat 2 tablespoons of the oil in a frying pan over low heat and cook the onion for 5 minutes, or until soft but not golden. Add the lamb and cook for 10 minutes, or until brown. Add the garlic and spices, tomato paste and tomatoes. Cook for 15 minutes. Add half the pine nuts and 2 tablespoons of the coriander. Season, then leave to cool.

4 Preheat the oven to 210°C (415°F/Gas 6–7). Grease two baking trays.

5 Knock down the dough, then turn out onto a floured surface. Form into eight portions and roll each one into an 12 x 18 cm (4½ x 7 inch) oval. Place on the trays. Divide the lamb mixture evenly among them and spread, leaving a small border. Sprinkle with the remaining pine nuts. Brush the edges with oil. Roll the uncovered dough over to cover the outer edges of the filling. Pinch the sides together at each end. Brush with oil. Bake for 15 minutes, or until golden. Sprinkle with coriander and serve with yoghurt.

SPANISH PIZZA

SERVES 4–6

BASE

2 teaspoons dried yeast

1 teaspoon caster (superfine) sugar

280 g (10 oz/2¼ cups) plain
(all-purpose) flour

TOPPING

10 English spinach leaves, shredded

1 tablespoon olive oil

2 garlic cloves, crushed

2 onions, chopped

400 g (14 oz) tin tomatoes, drained and
crushed

¼ teaspoon ground black pepper

12 pitted black olives, chopped

1 Preheat the oven to 210°C (415°F/Gas 6–7). Brush a 25 x 30 cm (10 x 12 inch) Swiss roll tin (jelly roll tin) with oil.

2 To make the base, combine the yeast, sugar and flour in a large bowl. Gradually add 250 ml (9 fl oz/1 cup) warm water and blend until smooth. Knead the dough on a lightly floured surface until smooth and elastic. Place in a lightly oiled bowl, cover with a tea towel (dish towel) and leave to rise in a warm position for 15 minutes, or until the dough has almost doubled in size.

3 To make the topping, put the spinach in a large saucepan, cover and cook on low heat for 3 minutes. Drain the spinach and cool. Squeeze out the excess moisture with your hands and set the spinach aside.

4 Heat the oil in a frying pan and add the garlic and onion. Cook over low heat for 5–6 minutes. Add the tomatoes and pepper and simmer gently for 5 minutes.

5 Punch the dough down, remove from the bowl and knead on a lightly floured board for 2–3 minutes. Roll the dough out and fit it in the tin. Spread with spinach, top with the tomato mixture and sprinkle the olives on top.

6 Bake for 25–30 minutes. Cut into small squares or fingers. The pizza can be served hot or cold.

PIZZETTE

MAKES 4

BASE

150 g (5½ oz/1 cup) plain (all-purpose)
   flour

150 g (5½ oz/1 cup) wholemeal plain
   (all-purpose) flour

2 teaspoons dry yeast

½ teaspoon sugar

½ teaspoon salt

2 tablespoons plain yoghurt

TOPPING

2 tablespoons tomato paste
   (concentrated purée)

1 garlic clove, crushed

1 teaspoon dried oregano

20 g (¾ oz) lean shaved ham

2 teaspoons grated mozzarella cheese

chopped rocket (arugula), to serve

olive oil, to serve

1 **To make the base,** sift the plain flour into a bowl, then add the wholemeal plain flour, dry yeast, sugar and salt. Make a well in the centre, add 125 ml (4 fl oz/½ cup) water and the yoghurt and mix to a dough. Knead on a lightly floured surface for 5 minutes, or until smooth and elastic. Cover with a tea towel (dish towel) and rest in a warm place for 20–30 minutes, or until doubled in size.

2 **Preheat the oven** to 200°C (400°F/Gas 6). Punch the dough down and knead for 30 seconds, then divide into four portions. Roll each portion into a 15 cm (6 inch) round and place on a baking tray.

3 **To make the topping,** combine the tomato paste, garlic, oregano and 1 tablespoon water. Spread the paste over each base then top with the ham and mozzarella. Bake for 12–15 minutes, or until crisp and golden on the edges. Just before serving, top with chopped rocket and drizzle with extra virgin olive oil.

PIZZA MARGHERITA

BASE

225 g (8 oz/1½ cups) white strong flour

1 teaspoon sugar

2 teaspoons dried yeast

½ teaspoon salt

1 tablespoon olive oil

90 ml (3 fl oz) milk

TOPPING

1 tablespoon olive oil

1 garlic clove, crushed

425 g (15 oz) tin crushed tomatoes

1 bay leaf

1 teaspoon chopped thyme

6 chopped basil leaves

polenta, to sprinkle

150 g (5½ oz) bocconcini cheese (fresh baby mozzarella cheese), thinly sliced

olive oil, extra, to drizzle

1 **To make the base**, put the flour, sugar, yeast and salt in a large bowl. Stir the olive oil with the milk and 4 tablespoons warm water and add to the bowl. Stir with a wooden spoon.

2 **Place on a lightly floured** work surface and knead for 5 minutes, or until soft and smooth. Lightly oil a bowl, add the dough and turn to coat in the oil. Leave in a warm place for 1 hour, or until doubled in size. Preheat the oven to 210°C (415°F/Gas 6–7).

3 **To make the topping**, heat the oil in a saucepan over medium heat, add the garlic and stir for 30 seconds. Add the tomatoes, bay leaf, thyme and basil and simmer, stirring occasionally, for 20–25 minutes, or until thick. Cool, then remove the bay leaf.

4 **Place the dough** on a floured work surface, punch down to expel the air and knead for 5 minutes. Shape into a ball and roll to 28–30 cm (11¼–12 inch) diameter.

5 **Oil a pizza tray** the size of the dough. Sprinkle the tray with polenta and place the dough on top. Spread sauce over the dough, leaving about a 2.5 cm (1 inch) border. Arrange the bocconcini slices over the top and drizzle with olive oil. Bake for 15 minutes, or until crisp and bubbling.

MUSHROOM POT PIES

SERVES 4

100 ml (3½ fl oz) olive oil

1 leek, white part only, sliced

1 garlic clove, crushed

1 kg (2 lb 4 oz) field mushrooms,
    roughly chopped

1 teaspoon chopped thyme

300 ml (10½ fl oz) cream

1 sheet puff pastry, thawed

1 egg yolk, beaten, to glaze

1 **Preheat oven** to 180°C (350°F/Gas 4). Heat 1 tablespoon oil in a frying pan over medium heat. Cook the leek and garlic for 5 minutes, or until the leek is soft and translucent. Transfer to a large saucepan.

2 **Heat the remaining oil** in the frying pan over high heat and cook the mushrooms in two batches, stirring frequently, for 5–7 minutes per batch, or until the mushrooms have released their juices and are soft. Transfer to the saucepan, then add the thyme.

3 **Place the saucepan** over high heat and stir in the cream until well mixed. Cook, stirring occasionally, for 7–8 minutes, or until the cream has reduced to a thick sauce. Remove from the heat and season well.

4 **Divide the filling** among four 310 ml (10¾ fl oz/1¼ cup) ramekins or ovenproof bowls. Cut pastry into rounds slightly larger than each dish. Brush the rim of the ramekins with a little of the egg yolk, place the pastry on top and press down to seal. Brush the top with the remaining egg yolk. Place the ramekins on a metal tray. Bake for 20–25 minutes, or until the pastry has risen and is golden brown. Great with mashed potato and a salad.

RUSTIC GREEK PIE

SERVES 4

450 g (1 lb) packet frozen spinach, thawed

1 large sheet ready-rolled shortcrust (pie) pastry, thawed

3 garlic cloves, finely chopped

150 g (5½ oz) haloumi cheese, grated

120 g (4¼ oz) feta cheese, crumbled

1 tablespoon oregano sprigs

2 eggs

3 tablespoons cream

lemon wedges, to serve

1 **Preheat the oven** to 200°C (400°F/Gas 6). Squeeze the excess liquid from the spinach.

2 **Place pastry** on a baking tray and spread the spinach in the middle, leaving about a 2.5 cm (1 inch) border around the edge. Sprinkle the garlic over the spinach and pile the haloumi and feta on top. Sprinkle with oregano and season well. Cut a short slit into each corner of the pastry, then tuck each side of pastry over to form a border around the filling.

3 **Lightly beat eggs** with the cream and carefully pour the egg mixture over the spinach filling. Bake for 25–30 minutes, or until the pastry is golden and the filling is set. Serve with the lemon wedges and a fresh green salad.

LAMB PIDE WITH GARLIC AND CHICKPEA PURÉE

SERVES 4

1 tablespoon lemon juice

1 teaspoon ground cumin

1 tablespoon olive oil

4 lamb fillets, trimmed

1 head of garlic

100 g (3½ oz/½ cup) tinned chickpeas, rinsed and drained

2 teaspoons lemon juice, extra

1 tablespoon plain yoghurt

4 x 100 g (3½ oz) pieces Turkish bread (pide)

2 tomatoes, sliced

1 very large handful rocket (arugular)

1 **Mix the lemon juice**, cumin, olive oil and some salt and pepper. Add the lamb fillets and leave to marinate for at least 1 hour.

2 **Preheat the oven** to 210°C (415°F/Gas 6–7). Wrap the bulb of garlic in foil, then roast for 20 minutes, or until soft. Cool, then squeeze out the pulp from each clove. Purée the pulp with the chickpeas, extra lemon juice and yoghurt in a food processor—add a little water to achieve a spreading consistency, if needed. Season.

3 **Grill (broil) or barbecue** the lamb for 3 minutes on each side, or until done to your liking. Grill or toast the Turkish bread, then slice through the middle and spread with the chickpea spread. Top with thin slices of the lamb, tomato and rocket leaves.

ARTICHOKE, OLIVE AND GOAT'S CHEESE PIZZA

SERVES 4

25 cm (10 inch) purchased pizza base

4 tablespoons Italian tomato pasta sauce

150 g (5½ oz) marinated artichokes, quartered

70 g (2½ oz) pitted Kalamata olives

1 clove, thinly sliced

50 g (2 oz) goat's cheese, crumbled

good-quality olive oil, to drizzle

2 tablespoons chopped oregano

1 Preheat the oven to 220°C (425°F/Gas 7). Place the pizza base on a baking tray, and spread with the tomato pasta sauce. Evenly scatter the artichoke pieces, olives and the garlic over the pasta sauce, then top with the crumbled goat's cheese.

2 Lightly drizzle the surface of the pizza with olive oil and bake for 20 minutes, or until golden. Sprinkle with oregano and season with salt and freshly ground black pepper. Cut into wedges and serve.

FRIED RICE WITH CHINESE BARBECUED PORK

SERVES 4

6 spring onions (scallions)

150 g (5½ oz) snow peas (mangetout)

200 g (7 oz) Chinese barbecued pork (char siu)

3 teaspoons sesame oil

2 eggs, lightly beaten

2 garlic cloves, finely chopped

555 g (1 lb 4 oz/3 cups) cold cooked white long-grain rice (see Note)

2 tablespoons soy sauce

1 Cut the spring onions and snow peas diagonally into very thin shreds. Cut the pork into thin slices.

2 Heat a wok until hot, add 1 teaspoon of the oil and swirl to coat the base. Add the egg and swirl over the base until just set. Turn over and cook for 30 seconds, or until just lightly browned, then remove from the wok. Allow the egg to cool slightly, then roll up and cut into 1 cm (½ inch) thick slices.

3 While the wok is still very hot, add the remaining oil, then the garlic, spring onion and snow peas and stir-fry for 1–2 minutes, or until slightly soft. Add the pork, rice, soy sauce and strips of omelette and toss until heated through and thoroughly combined—the soy sauce should turn the rice brown. Remove from the heat and serve immediately.

Note: Cook 200 g (7 oz/1 cup) long-grain rice in a large saucepan of boiling water. To cool, spread rice on a shallow tray and leave uncovered overnight in the refrigerator.

STEAMED RICE NOODLES

PORK FILLING

350 g (12 oz) Chinese barbecued pork (char siu), chopped

3 spring onions (scallions), finely chopped

2 tablespoons chopped coriander (cilantro) leaves

OR PRAWN FILLING

250 g (9 oz) small raw prawns (shrimp)

1 tablespoon oil

ground white pepper

3 spring onions (scallions), finely chopped

2 tablespoons chopped coriander (cilantro) leaves

OR VEGETABLE FILLING

300 g (10½ oz) Chinese broccoli (gai larn)

1 teaspoon light soy sauce

1 teaspoon sesame oil

2 spring onions (scallions), chopped

4 fresh rice noodle rolls, at room temperature

oyster sauce, to serve

1 To make the pork filling, combine the pork with the spring onion and coriander.

2 To make the prawn filling, peel the prawns and gently pull out the dark vein from each prawn back, starting from the head end. Heat a wok over high heat, add the oil and swirl to coat the base and side. When the oil is hot, add the prawns and stir-fry for 1 minute, or until they are pink and cooked through. Season with a little salt and ground white pepper. Add the spring onion and coriander and mix well.

3 To make the vegetable filling, wash the Chinese broccoli well. Discard any tough looking stems and chop the rest. Put on a plate in a steamer, cover with a lid and steam over a wok of simmering water for 3 minutes, or until the stems and leaves are just tender. Combine the Chinese broccoli with the soy sauce, sesame oil and spring onion.

4 Carefully unroll the rice noodle rolls (don't worry if they crack or tear a little at the sides). Trim each one into a neat rectangle about 15 x 18 cm (6 x 7 inch); you may be able to get two out of one roll if they are very large. Divide the filling among the rolls, then re-roll the noodles.

5 Put the rolls on a plate in a large steamer, cover and steam over a wok of simmering water for 5 minutes. Serve the rolls cut into pieces and drizzle with some oyster sauce.

DINNER

SPAGHETTI BOLOGNESE

SERVES 4

3 tablespoons butter

1 onion, finely chopped

2 garlic cloves, crushed

1 celery stalk, finely chopped

1 carrot, diced

50 g (2 oz) piece pancetta, diced

500 g (1 lb 2 oz) minced (ground) beef

1 tablespoon chopped oregano

250 ml (9 fl oz/1 cup) red wine

500 ml (17 fl oz/2 cups) beef stock

2 tablespoons tomato paste
(concentrated purée)

2 x 400 g (14 oz) tins crushed tomatoes

400 g (14 oz) spaghetti

3 tablespoons grated parmesan cheese

1 Melt the butter in a large saucepan, add the onion and cook over medium heat for 2–3 minutes, or until it starts to soften. Add the garlic, celery and carrot, and cook, stirring, over low heat, for 5 minutes. Increase the heat to high, add the pancetta, beef and oregano, and cook for 4–5 minutes, or until browned. Use a fork to break up any lumps.

2 Pour in the wine, reduce heat and simmer for about 5 minutes, or until it is absorbed. Add the stock, tomato paste and tomato, and season well. Cover with a lid and simmer for 1½ hours, stirring occasionally to prevent the sauce from catching on the bottom of the saucepan. Uncover and simmer for another hour, stirring occasionally.

3 Cook the spaghetti in a large saucepan of boiling water until al dente. Drain, divide among four serving plates and top with the sauce. Sprinkle with the parmesan cheese and serve.

PASTICCIO

SERVES 6

250 g (9 oz/1²/₃ cups) plain (all-purpose) flour

125 g (4½ oz) cold butter, chopped

3 tablespoons caster (superfine) sugar

1 egg yolk

150 g (5½ oz) bucatini or penne

FILLING

2 tablespoons olive oil

1 onion, chopped

2 garlic cloves, finely chopped

500 g (1 lb 2 oz) minced (ground) beef

150 g (5½ oz) chicken livers

2 tomatoes, chopped

125 ml (4 fl oz/½ cup) red wine

125 ml (4 fl oz/½ cup) rich beef stock

1 tablespoon chopped oregano

¼ teaspoon freshly grated nutmeg

100 g (3½ oz/1 cup) parmesan cheese

BÉCHAMEL SAUCE

3 tablespoons butter

2 tablespoons plain (all-purpose) flour

375 ml (12 fl oz/1½ cups) cold milk

1 Put the flour, butter, sugar and egg yolk in a food processor with 1 tablespoon water. Process lightly until the mixture forms a ball, adding more water if necessary. Lightly knead the dough on a floured surface until smooth. Wrap in plastic wrap and refrigerate.

2 To make the filling, heat oil in a heavy-based saucepan and cook onion and garlic until softened and lightly golden. Increase the heat, add the beef and cook until browned, breaking up any lumps with a fork. Add the livers, tomato, red wine, stock, oregano and nutmeg, then season well. Cook the sauce over high heat until it boils. Reduce to a simmer and cook, covered, for 40 minutes, then cool. Stir in the parmesan.

3 To make the béchamel sauce, heat the butter in a saucepan over low heat. Add the flour and stir for 1 minute, or until the mixture is golden and smooth. Remove from the heat and gradually stir in the milk. Return to the heat and stir constantly until the sauce boils and begins to thicken. Simmer for another minute. Season to taste.

4 Cook the bucatini in a saucepan of rapidly boiling salted water until al dente. Drain and cool.

5 Preheat the oven to 160°C (315°F/Gas 2–3). Lightly grease a 23 cm (9 inch) deep pie dish. Divide dough into two and roll out one piece to fit the base of the prepared dish, overlapping the sides. Spoon about half of the meat mixture into the dish, top with the bucatini and slowly spoon the béchamel sauce over the top, allowing it to seep down and coat the bucatini. Top with the remaining meat. Roll out the remaining dough and cover the pie. Trim the edges and pinch lightly to seal. Bake for 50–55 minutes, or until dark golden brown and crisp. Set aside for 15 minutes before cutting.

BAKED CHEESE AND SPINACH CANNELLONI

SERVES 4

TOMATO SAUCE

2 tablespoons olive oil

1 large onion, finely chopped

2 garlic cloves, finely chopped

1.25 kg (2 lb 12 oz) tinned tomatoes,
    roughly chopped

2 rosemary sprigs

2 bay leaves

2 tablespoons tomato paste
    (concentrated purée)

500 g (1 lb 2 oz) English spinach

150 g (5½ oz) feta cheese, crumbled

150 g (5½ oz) ricotta cheese

50 g (2 oz/½ cup) parmesan cheese

2 tablespoons finely chopped mint

2 eggs, lightly beaten

2 tablespoons pine nuts, toasted

16 instant cannelloni tubes

200 g (7 oz) mozzarella cheese,
    finely grated

1 **To make the tomato sauce**, heat the olive oil in a large pan. Add the onion and garlic and cook over medium heat until the onion is soft. Add the tomato, herbs and tomato paste and mix thoroughly. Bring to the boil, reduce the heat and simmer for 25–30 minutes until the sauce is thick. Season to taste. Remove the bay leaves and rosemary sprigs and discard.

2 **Preheat the oven** to 200°C (400°F/Gas 6). Wash and remove the stems from the spinach. Steam until just wilted. Drain thoroughly and chop roughly. Combine the spinach with the ricotta and parmesan cheeses, mint, beaten eggs, pine nuts and season. Mix thoroughly. Using a small spoon or knife, carefully fill the cannelloni tubes.

3 **Spoon some tomato** sauce over the base of a large, shallow baking dish. Arrange cannelloni shells on top. Cover with remaining tomato sauce and mozzarella. Bake for 30–40 minutes, or until the top is golden and pasta is tender.

CLASSIC LASAGNE

SERVES 8

2 tablespoons oil

30 g (1 oz) butter

1 large onion, finely chopped

1 carrot, finely chopped

1 celery stalk, finely chopped

500 g (1 lb 2 oz) minced (ground) beef

150 g (5½ oz) chicken livers, finely chopped (see Note)

250 ml (9 fl oz/1 cup) tomato passata (puréed tomatoes)

250 ml (9 fl oz/1 cup) red wine

2 tablespoons chopped flat-leaf (Italian) parsley

375 g (13 oz) fresh lasagne sheets

100 g (3½ oz/1 cup) grated parmesan cheese

BÉCHAMEL SAUCE

60 g (2¼ oz) butter

4 tablespoons plain (all-purpose) flour

560 ml (19¼ fl oz/2¼ cups) milk

½ teaspoon freshly grated nutmeg

1 Heat the oil and butter in a heavy-based frying pan and cook the onion, carrot and celery over medium heat until softened, stirring constantly. Increase heat, add beef and brown well, breaking up any lumps with a fork. Add chicken livers and cook until they change colour. Add the tomato passata, wine, parsley, and season to taste. Bring to the boil, reduce heat and simmer 45 minutes; set aside.

2 To make béchamel sauce, melt the butter in a saucepan over low heat. Add the flour and stir for 1 minute. Remove from the heat and gradually stir in the milk. Return to the heat and stir constantly until the sauce boils and begins to thicken. Simmer for another minute. Add the nutmeg and season to taste. Place a piece of plastic wrap on the surface of the sauce to prevent a skin forming, and set aside.

3 Cut the lasagne sheets to fit into a deep, rectangular ovenproof dish.

4 To assemble, preheat the oven to 180°C (350°F/Gas 4). Grease the ovenproof dish. Spread a thin layer of the meat sauce over the base and follow with a thin layer of béchamel. If the béchamel has cooled and become too thick, warm it gently to make spreading easier. Lay the lasagne sheets on top, gently pressing to push out any air. Continue the layers, finishing with béchamel. Sprinkle with parmesan and bake for 35–40 minutes, or until golden brown. Cool for 15 minutes before cutting.

Notes: Instant lasagne can be used instead of fresh. Follow the manufacturer's instructions. If you prefer, you can leave out the chicken livers and increase the amount of beef.

CHICKEN AND MUSHROOM RISOTTO

SERVES 4

1.25 litres (44 fl oz/5 cups) vegetable or chicken stock

2 tablespoons olive oil

300 g (10½ oz) chicken breast fillets, cut into 1.5 cm (½ inch) wide strips

250 g (9 oz) small button mushrooms, halved

pinch of nutmeg

2 garlic cloves, crushed

20 g (¾ oz) butter

1 small onion, finely chopped

375 g (17 fl oz) arborio rice

170 ml (5½ fl oz/⅔ cup) dry white wine

3 tablespoons sour cream

3 tablespoons finely chopped flat-leaf (Italian) parsley

45 g (1½ oz) grated parmesan cheese

1 **Bring stock to the boil**, reduce heat and keep at a simmer.

2 **Heat the oil** in a large saucepan. Cook the chicken over high heat for 3–4 minutes or until golden brown. Add the mushrooms and cook for 1–2 minutes more, or until starting to brown. Stir in the nutmeg and garlic, and season with salt and pepper. Cook for 30 seconds then remove from the pan and set aside.

3 **Melt the butter** in the same pan and cook the onion over low heat for 5–6 minutes. Add the rice, stir to coat, then add the wine. Once wine is absorbed, reduce the heat and add 125 ml (4 fl oz/½ cup) of the stock. When it is absorbed, add

another 125 ml (4 fl oz/½ cup). Continue adding stock for 20–25 minutes, or until all the stock has been used and the rice is creamy. Add the mushrooms and the chicken with the last of the stock.

4 **Remove the pan** from the heat, and stir in the sour cream, parsley and parmesan cheese. Check the seasoning then cover and leave for 2 minutes before serving.

SERVES 4

1.25 litres (44 fl oz/5 cups) chicken stock

bouquet garni (1 sprig thyme, 1 bay leaf,
    2 stalks flat-leaf/Italian parsley)

2 tablespoons olive oil

1 onion, chopped

1 small celery stalk, chopped

60 g (2¼ oz) pancetta, chopped

250 g (9 oz) arborio rice

300 g (10½ oz/2 cups) frozen baby peas

60 g (2¼ oz) unsalted butter

80 g (3 oz) grated parmesan cheese

shaved parmesan cheese, to serve

1 **Place the stock** and bouquet garni in a large saucepan with 750 ml (26 fl oz/3 cups) water. Bring to the boil, then reduce the heat and simmer.

2 **Heat the oil** in a large frying pan, add the onion, celery and pancetta, and cook for 3–5 minutes, or until the onion is soft. Add the rice and stir for 1 minute, or until coated.

3 **Remove the bouquet** garni and add 125 ml (4 fl oz/ ½ cup) hot stock to the rice, stirring constantly until all the stock is absorbed. Add another 125 ml (4 fl oz/½ cup) stock and stir until all the stock is absorbed. Add the peas. Continue adding stock, 125 ml (4 fl oz/½ cup) at a time, stirring, for 20–25 minutes, or until the rice is tender. The texture should be a little wetter than risotto, but not too soupy. Remove from the heat and stir in the butter and grated parmesan cheese. Season. Garnish with shaved parmesan cheese

HAM AND CHEESE PASTA BAKE

SERVES 4

1½ tablespoons olive oil

1 onion, finely chopped

300 g (10½ oz) leg ham, sliced 3 mm
(⅛ in) thick and cut into 5 cm (2 inch)
lengths

600 ml (21 fl oz) cream

300 g (10½ oz/2 cups) cooked fresh
peas or frozen peas, thawed

375 g (13 oz) conchiglione (pasta shells)

3 tablespoons roughly chopped basil

250 g (9 oz/2 cups) grated mature
cheddar cheese

1 **Preheat the oven** to 200°C (400°F/Gas 6) and lightly
grease a 2.5 litre (87 fl oz/10 cup) ovenproof ceramic dish.
Heat 1 tablespoon of the oil in a frying pan over medium heat
and cook the onion, stirring frequently for 5 minutes, or until
soft. Add the remaining oil, then the ham and cook, stirring,
for 1 minute. Pour the cream into the pan, bring to the boil,
then reduce the heat and simmer for 6 minutes. Add the peas
and cook for another 2–4 minutes, or until the mixture has
reduced and thickened slightly. Season with freshly ground
black pepper.

2 **Meanwhile**, cook the pasta in a large saucepan of rapidly
boiling salted water according to the packet instructions until
al dente. Drain and return to the pan.

3 **Add the cream** sauce to the pasta, then the basil and
three-quarters of the cheese. Stir well and season. Transfer the
mixture to the prepared dish, sprinkle on the remaining cheese
and bake for 20 minutes, or until the top is golden brown.

Note: Other pasta shapes such as spirals, farfalle, fusilli or
macaroni are suitable for this dish.

VEGETABLE BAKE

SERVES 4

400 g (14 oz) potatoes, thinly sliced
    lengthways

60 g (2¼ oz) butter, melted

1½–2 teaspoons finely chopped thyme

400 g (14 oz) pumpkin (winter squash),
    thinly sliced

300 g (10½ oz) zucchini (courgettes),
    thinly sliced lengthways

250 ml (9 fl oz/1 cup) tomato pasta
    sauce

50 g (2 oz/½ cup) grated parmesan
    cheese

1 **Preheat oven** to 170°C (325°F/Gas 3). Grease a 1.5 litre (52 fl oz/6 cup) rectangular ovenproof dish. Combine the potato with one-third each of the butter and thyme. Season, then place in the base of the prepared dish.

2 **Combine the pumpkin** and another third of the butter and thyme. Season and press onto the potato. Combine the zucchini with the remaining butter and thyme. Season and press onto the pumpkin.

3 **Spread the pasta** sauce evenly over the top and cover with greased foil. Bake for 45 minutes, remove the foil and sprinkle with the grated parmesan cheese. Bake for another 15 minutes, or until the top is golden brown and the vegetables are cooked through. Can be served with a salad and crusty bread, if desired.

MEXICAN CHICKEN BAKE

SERVES 4

165 g (5¾ oz/¾ cup) short-grain white rice

300 g (10½ oz) tin red kidney beans, rinsed and drained

3½ tablespoons chopped coriander (cilantro) leaves

1 tablespoon oil

600 g (1 lb 5 oz) boneless, skinless chicken thighs, unrolled

2 x 200 g (7 oz) jars spicy taco sauce

250 g (9 oz/2 cups) grated cheddar cheese

125 g (4½ oz/½ cup) sour cream

1 Preheat the oven to 180°C (350°F/Gas 4). Lightly grease a 7 cm (2¾ inch) deep, 21 cm (8 inch) round ceramic casserole dish. Bring a large saucepan of water to the boil, add the rice and cook for 10–12 minutes, stirring occasionally. Drain.

2 In the prepared dish, combine beans and 1½ tablespoons of the coriander, then add the rice and toss together. Lightly press the mixture so the beans are mixed into the rice and the mixture is flat.

3 Heat the oil in a large frying pan over medium–high heat. Sauté the chicken thighs for 3 minutes, then turn over. Add the spicy taco sauce, and cook for another 3 minutes.

4 To assemble, spread half the cheese over the rice. Arrange the thighs and sauce on top in a star shape, sprinkle with 1½ tablespoons coriander, then sprinkle with cheese. Cover with foil.

5 Bake for 35–40 minutes, or until mixture is bubbling and the cheese is melted and slightly browned—remove the foil for the last 5 minutes. Cut into four servings with a knife and scoop out carefully, keeping the layers intact. Serve sprinkled with the remaining coriander and a dollop of sour cream.

TORTILLA PIE

SERVES 4

1 tablespoon oil

500 g (1 lb 2 oz) lean minced (ground) beef

35 g (1¼ oz) packet taco seasoning mix

420 g (15 oz) tin Mexican chilli beans, rinsed and drained

8 flour tortillas

250 g (2 cups) grated cheddar cheese

300 g (10½ oz) Mexican tomato salsa

150 g (5½ oz) sour cream

1 avocado, diced

1 **Preheat the oven** to 180°C (350°F/Gas 4). Grease a 23 cm (9 inch) pie dish. Heat the oil in a large non-stick frying pan. Add the beef and cook for 5 minutes, or until brown, breaking up the lumps with the back of a spoon. Drain off the excess oil. Add the seasoning mix and cook for 5 minutes. Stir in the beans until heated through.

2 **Lay a tortilla** in the base of the pie dish. Spread 125 g (4½ oz/½ cup) of the beef mixture on top, then sprinkle with 3 tablespoons cheese and 1 tablespoon salsa. Continue the layering with the remaining tortillas, beef mixture, cheese and salsa, ending with a tortilla sprinkled with a little cheese—it should end up looking like a dome shape.

3 **Bake for 15 minutes**, or until all the cheese has melted and browned. Cool slightly, cut into wedges and top with a dollop of sour cream and the diced avocado. Serve with a tomato salad, if desired.

ROASTED LAMB SHANKS IN TOMATO SAUCE ON POLENTA

SERVES 4

2 tablespoons olive oil

1 large red onion, sliced

4 French-trimmed lamb shanks
(about 250 g/9 oz each)

2 garlic cloves, crushed

400 g can (14 oz) chopped tomatoes

125 ml (4 fl oz/½ cup) red wine

2 teaspoons chopped fresh rosemary

¼ teaspoon salt

¼ teaspoon freshly ground black pepper

150 g (5½ oz/1 cup) instant polenta

50 g (2 oz) butter

50 g (2 oz/½ cup) grated parmesan
cheese

1   **Preheat the oven** to 160°C (315°F/Gas 2–3). Heat the oil in a 4-litre (140 fl oz/16 cup) flameproof casserole dish over medium heat and sauté the onion for 3–4 minutes, or until softening and becoming transparent. Add the lamb shanks and cook for 2–3 minutes, or until lightly browned. Add the garlic, tomato and wine, then bring to the boil and cook for 3–4 minutes.

2   **Stir in the rosemary.** Season with the salt and pepper

3   **Cover and bake for 2 hours.** Uncover, return to the oven and simmer for another 15 minutes, or until the lamb just starts to fall off the bone. Check periodically that the sauce is not too dry, adding water, if needed.

4   **About 20 minutes** before serving, bring 1 litre (35 fl oz/ 4 cups) water to the boil in a saucepan. Add the polenta in a thin stream, whisking continuously, then reduce the heat to very low. Simmer for 8–10 minutes, or until thick and coming away from the side of the saucepan. Stir in the butter and parmesan cheese. To serve, spoon the polenta onto serving plates, top with the shanks and a little sauce from the casserole over the shanks.

SAUSAGE AND BEAN HOTPOT WITH SWEET POTATO

SERVES 4

1 kg (2 lb 4 oz) spicy Italian-style sausages

2 garlic cloves, roughly chopped

2 x 400 g (14 oz) tins cannellini beans

2 x 425 g (15 oz) tins crushed tomatoes

2 teaspoons dijon mustard

750 g (1 lb 10 oz) orange sweet potato, cut into 2.5 cm (1 inch) cubes

2 tablespoons olive oil

2 tablespoons coarsely chopped flat-leaf (Italian) parsley

1 **Preheat the oven** to 200°C (400°F/Gas 6). Cook sausages in a large frying pan over medium heat for 5–7 minutes, or until golden. Cut into 5 cm (2 in) pieces and place in a 4-litre (140 fl oz/16 cup) casserole dish. Add the garlic, beans, tomato, mustard and 2 tablespoons water to the dish and season with pepper. Stir well and cover with a lid. Place in the oven.

2 **Meanwhile**, toss the sweet potato with the oil and place snugly in a baking dish. Sprinkle with salt. Place in the oven with the casserole dish and bake for 25 minutes. Uncover the casserole dish and bake for another 10–15 minutes, or until the hotpot is golden and bubbling and the sweet potato is soft and lightly golden brown. Serve the hotpot garnished with the parsley and the sweet potato on the side.

CHICKEN GUMBO

SERVES 4–6

30 g (1 oz) butter

2 slices bacon, thinly sliced

1 small onion, chopped

1 small green capsicum (pepper), seed and membrane removed, diced

2 garlic cloves, chopped

¼ teaspoon cayenne pepper

600 g (1 lb 5 oz) boneless, skinless chicken breast, cubed

¼ teaspoon saffron threads, soaked in 2 tablespoons warm water

1 tablespoon brandy

1 tablespoon tomato paste (concentrated purée)

2 tablespoons plain (all-purpose) flour

1 litre (35 fl oz/4 cups) chicken stock

150 g (5½ oz/¾ cup) basmati rice

1 tablespoon olive oil

400 g (14 oz) raw small prawns (shrimp), peeled, deveined, tails intact

300 g (10½ oz) okra, thickly sliced

2 tablespoons cream

3 tablespoons chopped flat-leaf (Italian) parsley

½ teaspoon Tabasco sauce

1   Melt the butter in a large saucepan over medium heat, add the bacon, onion, capsicum, garlic, cayenne and chicken, and cook, stirring, for 5–8 minutes, or until light golden.

2   Stir in the saffron and soaking liquid, the brandy, tomato paste and flour, and cook, stirring constantly, for 3 minutes.

3   Gradually add the stock and bring to the boil. Add the rice, then reduce the heat to low and simmer gently for 10 minutes.

4   Meanwhile, heat the olive oil in a separate saucepan, add the prawns and okra, and toss quickly together for about 2 minutes, or until the prawns change colour. Add to the gumbo, then stir in cream, parsley and Tabasco, and heat for 1–2 minutes. Serve in deep bowls with corn bread.

CHICKEN AND MUSHROOM PILAU

SERVES 4–6

300 g (10½ oz/1½ cups) basmati rice

2 tablespoons oil

1 large onion, chopped

3–4 garlic cloves, crushed

1 tablespoon finely chopped ginger

500 g (1 lb 2 oz) chicken tenderloin fillets, trimmed and cut into small pieces

300 g (10½ oz) Swiss brown mushrooms, sliced

90 g (3¼ oz/¾ cup) slivered almonds, toasted

1½–2 teaspoons garam masala, dry roasted

125 g (4½ oz/½ cup) plain yoghurt

1 tablespoon finely chopped coriander (cilantro) leaves

coriander (cilantro) leaves, extra, to garnish

1 Rinse the rice under cold water until the water runs clear. Drain and leave for 30 minutes. Heat the oil in a large saucepan and stir in the onion, garlic and ginger. Reduce the heat to medium and cook, covered, for 5 minutes, or until the onion has browned. Increase the heat to high, add the chicken and cook, stirring, for 3–4 minutes, or until the chicken is lightly browned. Stir in the sliced mushrooms, almonds and garam masala. Cook, covered, for another 3 minutes, or until the mushrooms are soft. Uncover and cook without stirring for 2 minutes, or until the liquid has evaporated.

2 Remove the chicken from the pan. Add the rice and stir for 30 seconds, or until well coated in the mushroom and onion mixture. Pour in 375 ml (13 fl oz/1½ cups) water and bring to the boil, stirring frequently, for 2 minutes, or until most of the water evaporates. Return the chicken to the pan. Cover, reduce the heat to low and steam for 15 minutes, or until the rice is cooked.

3 Combine the yoghurt and chopped coriander. Fluff the rice with a fork, and divide among serving bowls. Top with a dollop of the yoghurt mixture and garnish with coriander leaves.

PUMPKIN RISOTTO

SERVES 4–6

600 g (1 lb 5 oz) pumpkin (winter squash), cut into 1 cm (½ inch) cubes

3 tablespoons olive oil

500 ml (17 fl oz/2 cups) vegetable stock

1 onion, finely chopped

2 garlic cloves, finely chopped

1 tablespoon chopped rosemary

440 g (15½ oz/2 cups) arborio rice

125 ml (4 fl oz/½ cup) dry white wine

30 g (1 oz) butter

4 tablespoons grated parmesan cheese

3 tablespoons finely chopped flat-leaf (Italian) parsley

1 **Preheat the oven** to moderately hot 200°C (400°F/Gas 6). Toss the pieces of pumpkin in 2 tablespoons of the oil, place in a baking dish and roast for 30 minutes, or until tender and golden. Turn the pumpkin halfway through the cooking time.

2 **Heat the stock** and 750 ml (26 fl oz/3 cups) water in a saucepan, cover and keep at a low simmer.

3 **Heat the remaining oil** in a large saucepan and cook the onion, garlic and rosemary, stirring, over low heat for 5 minutes, or until the onion is cooked but not browned. Add the rice and stir to coat. Stir in the wine for 2–3 minutes, or until absorbed.

4 **Add 125 ml (4 fl oz/½ cup) stock**, stirring constantly over medium heat until all the liquid is absorbed. Continue adding the stock 125 ml (4 fl oz/½ cup) at a time, stirring constantly, for 20 minutes, or until all the stock is absorbed and the rice is tender and creamy. Season to taste with salt and black pepper, and stir in the pumpkin, butter, parmesan cheese and parsley. Serve immediately.

SWEET POTATO AND SAGE RISOTTO

SERVES 4

8 slices prosciutto

100 ml (3½ fl oz) extra virgin olive oil

1 red onion, cut into thin wedges

600 g (1 lb 5 oz) orange sweet potato, peeled, cut into 2.5 cm (1 inch) cubes

440 g (15½ oz/2 cups) arborio rice

1.25 litres (44 fl oz/5 cups) hot chicken stock

75 g (2½ oz/¾ cup) shredded parmesan cheese

3 tablespoons shredded fresh sage

1 Place the prosciutto slices on a tray and cook under a hot grill (broiler) for 1–2 minutes each side, or until crispy.

2 Heat 3 tablespoons oil in a large saucepan, add the onion and cook over medium heat for 2–3 minutes, or until softened. Add the sweet potato and rice, and stir through until well coated in the oil.

3 Add 125 ml (4 fl oz/½ cup), hot chicken stock, stirring constantly over medium heat until the liquid is absorbed. Continue adding more stock, 125 ml (4 fl oz/½ cup at a time, stirring constantly for 20–25 minutes, or until all the stock is absorbed, and the rice is tender and creamy. Stir in shredded parmesan and 2 tablespoons of sage. Season. Spoon into four bowls and drizzle with the remaining oil. Break the prosciutto into pieces and sprinkle over the top with the remaining sage. Top with extra shaved parmesan cheese, if desired.

PORK AND CARAWAY PILAFF

SERVES 4

2 tablespoons oil

400 g (14 oz) diced lean pork

1 large onion, diced

2 garlic cloves, crushed

1 tablespoon caraway seeds

300 g (10½ oz/1½ cups) basmati rice, rinsed until water runs clear

750 ml (26 fl oz/3 cups) chicken stock

125 g (4½ oz/½ cup) plain yoghurt

2 tablespoons chopped coriander (cilantro) leaves

1 **Heat the oil** in a large frying pan over medium–high heat. Cook the pork until brown, then remove from the pan.

2 **Add onion** and garlic to the pan and cook for 3–5 minutes, or until the onion has softened. Add the caraway seeds and rice and cook for 2 minutes, stirring frequently, or until the rice is glossy and spices fragrant.

3 **Add the pork** and pour in the stock. Bring to the boil, then reduce heat to a simmer. Cover and cook for 15–20 minutes, or until the rice and pork is cooked.

4 **Season to taste** and serve topped with a dollop of yoghurt and the coriander.

LAMB PILAFF

SERVES 4

1 large eggplant (aubergine), cut into 1 cm (½ inch) cubes

125 ml (4 fl oz/½ cup) olive oil

1 large onion, finely chopped

1 teaspoon ground cinnamon

2 teaspoons ground cumin

1 teaspoon ground coriander

300 g (10½ oz/1½ cups) long-grain rice

500 ml (17 fl oz/2 cups) chicken or vegetable stock

500 g (1 lb 2 oz) minced (ground) lamb

½ teaspoon allspice

2 tablespoons olive oil, extra

2 tomatoes, cut into wedges

3 tablespoons pistachios, toasted

2 tablespoons currants

2 tablespoons chopped coriander (cilantro) leaves, to garnish

1 **Put the eggplant** in a colander, sprinkle with salt and leave for 1 hour. Rinse and squeeze dry. Heat 2 tablespoons of the oil in a large, deep frying pan with a lid, add the eggplant and cook over medium heat for 8–10 minutes. Drain on paper towels.

2 **Heat the remaining oil**, add the onion and cook for 4–5 minutes, or until soft. Stir in half each of the cinnamon, cumin and ground coriander. Add the rice and stir to coat, then add the stock, season and bring to the boil. Reduce the heat and simmer, covered, for 15 minutes.

3 **Put the lamb** in a bowl with the allspice and remaining cumin, cinnamon and ground coriander. Season with salt and pepper, and mix. Roll into balls the size of macadamia nuts. Heat the extra oil in the frying pan and cook the meatballs in batches over medium heat for 5 minutes each batch. Drain on paper towels.

4 **Add the tomato** to the pan and cook, for 3–5 minutes, or until golden. Remove from the pan. Stir eggplant, pistachios, currants and meatballs through the rice. Serve the pilaff with the tomato and coriander.

PASTA WITH BEEF RAGÙ

SERVES 4

100 g (3½ oz) streaky bacon or pancetta (not trimmed), finely chopped

1 onion, finely chopped

3 garlic cloves, crushed

1 bay leaf

800 g (1 lb 12 oz) lean minced (ground) beef

500 ml (17 fl oz/2 cups) red wine

4 tablespoons tomato paste (concentrated purée)

400 g (14 oz) tagliatelle

freshly grated parmesan cheese, to garnish

1 Heat a large deep frying pan (preferably stainless steel or non-coated). Add the bacon or pancetta and cook over medium–high heat for 2 minutes, or until soft and just starting to brown. Add onion, garlic and bay leaf and cook 2 minutes, or until the onion is soft and just starting to brown.

2 Add the beef and stir for about 4 minutes, or until the beef browns, breaking up any lumps with the back of a wooden spoon. Add the wine, tomato paste and 250 ml (9 fl oz/1 cup) water and stir well. Bring to the boil, then reduce the heat and simmer, covered, for 40 minutes. Remove the lid and cook for another 40 minutes, or until reduced to a thick, glossy sauce.

3 About 20 minutes before the ragù is ready, bring a large saucepan of salted water to a rapid boil and cook the pasta until al dente. Drain. Serve sauce over the pasta and garnish with a little grated parmesan cheese.

SHEPHERD'S PIE WITH GARLIC MASH

SERVES 4

1½ tablespoons oil

1 large onion, finely chopped

1 carrot, finely diced

8 garlic cloves, peeled

750 g lean minced (ground) lamb

375 ml (13 fl oz/1½ cups) Italian tomato pasta sauce

300 ml (10½ fl oz) beef stock

800 g (1 lb 12 oz) potatoes, cut into large chunks

30 g (1 oz) butter

1 Heat oil in a large saucepan over medium heat. Add the onion and carrot and cook for 5 minutes, or until soft. Crush 2 garlic cloves and sauté with the onion for another minute. Add the lamb and stir well, breaking up any lumps with the back of a wooden spoon. Cook for 5 minutes, or until browned and cooked through. Spoon off any excess fat, add the tomato pasta sauce and 250 ml (9 fl oz/1 cup) stock. Cover and bring to the boil. Reduce the heat to medium–low and simmer for 25 minutes. Then uncover and cook for a further 20 minutes, or until the sauce thickens. Preheat the oven to 200°C (400°F/Gas 6).

2 Meanwhile, cook the potato in a saucepan of boiling water with the remaining garlic for 15–20 minutes, or until tender. Drain well, return to the pan over low heat, stirring to evaporate any excess water. Remove from heat, add the butter and remaining stock and mash until smooth. Season.

3 Transfer the lamb mixture to a 1.5 litre (52 fl oz/6 cup) ovenproof ceramic dish. Spread the potato over the top. Use a fork to swirl the surface. Bake for 40 minutes, or until the potato is golden brown.

SEAFOOD PAELLA

SERVES 6

2 tomatoes, peeled

500 g (1 lb 2 oz) raw prawns (shrimp), peeled and deveined, with tails intact

250 g (9 oz) black mussels, scrubbed and beards removed

200 g (7 oz) squid rings

3 tablespoons olive oil

1 large onion, diced

3 garlic cloves, finely chopped

1 small red capsicum (pepper), seeded and membrane removed, thinly sliced

1 small red chilli, seeded and chopped (optional)

2 teaspoons paprika

1 teaspoon ground turmeric

1 teaspoon salt

1 tablespoon tomato paste (concentrated purée)

440 g (15½ oz/2 cups) paella rice or risotto rice

125 ml (4 fl oz/½ cup) dry white wine

¼ teaspoon saffron threads, soaked in 3 tablespoons hot water

1.25 litres (44 fl oz/5 cups) fish stock

300 g (10½ oz) skinless firm white fish fillets, cut into 2.5 cm (1 inch) cubes

3 tablespoons chopped flat-leaf (Italian) parsley, to serve

lemon wedges, to serve

1 Cut each tomato in half, remove the seeds and finely chop the flesh.

2 Scrub the mussels with a stiff brush and pull out the hairy beards. Discard any broken mussels or open ones that don't close when tapped on the bench. Rinse well. Refrigerate covered, until ready to use.

3 Heat the oil in a paella pan or large, deep frying pan with a lid. Add the onion, garlic, capsicum and chilli to the pan and cook over medium heat for 2 minutes, or until the onion and capsicum are soft. Add the paprika, turmeric and stir-fry for 1–2 minutes, or until fragrant. Add the chopped tomato and cook for 5 minutes, or until softened. Add the tomato paste. Stir in the rice until well coated.

4 Pour in the wine and simmer until almost absorbed. Add the saffron and its soaking liquid and all the fish stock. Bring to the boil, then reduce the heat and simmer for 20 minutes, or until almost all the liquid is absorbed into the rice. There is no need to stir the rice, but you may occasionally wish to fluff it up with a fork to separate the grains.

5 Add the mussels, poking the shells into the rice, cover and cook for 1–2 minutes over low heat. Add prawns and cook for 2–3 minutes. Add fish, cover and cook for 3 minutes. Add the squid rings and cook for 1–2 minutes. By this time, the mussels should have opened — discard any unopened ones. The prawns should be pink and the fish should flake easily when tested with a fork. The squid should be white, moist and tender. Cook for another 2–3 minutes if seafood is not quite cooked, but avoid overcooking. Remove from the heat, cover loosely with foil and set aside for 5–10 minutes. Serve with parsley and lemon wedges.

MOUSSAKA

SERVES 6

2 large tomatoes

1.5 kg (3 lb 5 oz) eggplant (aubergine), cut into 5 mm (¼ inch) slices

125 ml (4 fl oz/½ cup) olive oil

2 onions, finely chopped

2 large garlic cloves, crushed

½ teaspoon ground allspice

1 teaspoon ground cinnamon

750 g (1 lb 10 oz) minced (ground) lamb

2 tablespoons tomato paste (concentrated purée)

125 ml (4 fl oz/½ cup) dry white wine

3 tablespoons chopped flat-leaf (Italian) parsley

CHEESE SAUCE

60 g (2¼ oz) butter

60 g (2¼ oz/½ cup) plain (all-purpose) flour

625 ml (21½ fl oz/2½ cups) milk

a pinch of nutmeg

4 tablespoons grated kefalotyri or parmesan cheese

2 eggs, lightly beaten

1 **Cut each tomato** in half, scoop out the seeds and finely chop the flesh. Lay the eggplant on a tray, sprinkle with salt and leave for 30 minutes. Rinse under water and pat dry.

2 **Heat 2 tablespoons** of the olive oil in a frying pan, add the eggplant in batches and cook for 1–2 minutes each side, or until golden and soft. Add a little more oil when needed. Heat 1 tablespoon of the olive oil in a large saucepan, add the onion and cook over medium heat for 5 minutes. Add the garlic, allspice and cinnamon and cook for 30 seconds. Add the lamb and cook for 5 minutes, or until browned, breaking up any lumps with the back of a spoon. Add the tomato, tomato paste and wine, and simmer over low heat for 30 minutes, or until the liquid has evaporated. Stir in the chopped parsley and season to taste. Preheat the oven to 180°C (350°F/Gas 4).

3 **To make the cheese sauce,** melt the butter in a saucepan over low heat. Stir in the flour and cook for 1 minute, or until pale and foaming. Remove the saucepan from the heat and gradually stir in the milk and nutmeg. Return the saucepan to the heat and stir constantly until the sauce boils and thickens. Reduce the heat and simmer for 2 minutes. Stir in 1 tablespoon of the cheese until well combined.

4 **Line the base** of a 3 litre (105 fl oz/12 cup) ovenproof dish, which measures 25 x 30 cm (10 x 12 inch), with a third of the eggplant. Spoon half the meat sauce over it and cover with another layer of eggplant. Spoon the remaining meat sauce over the top and cover with the remaining eggplant. Stir the egg into the cheese sauce. Spread the sauce over the top of the eggplant and sprinkle with the remaining cheese. Bake for 1 hour. Leave to stand for 10 minutes before slicing.

CLASSIC JAMBALAYA

SERVES 4–6

2 tablespoons olive oil

1 large red onion, finely chopped

1 garlic clove, crushed

2 slices back bacon, finely chopped

300 g (10½ oz/1½ cups) long-grain rice

1 red capsicum (pepper), seeded and membrane removed, diced

150 g (5½ oz) ham, chopped

400 g (14 oz) tin chopped tomatoes

400 g (14 oz) tomato passata or tomato pasta sauce

1 teaspoon worcestershire sauce

dash of Tabasco sauce

½ teaspoon dried thyme

30 g (1 oz/½ cup) chopped parsley

150 g (5½ oz) cooked, peeled, small prawns (shrimp)

4 spring onions (scallions), thinly sliced

1 **Heat the oil** in a large saucepan over medium heat. Add the onion, garlic and bacon and cook, stirring, for 5 minutes, or until the onion is softened but not browned. Stir in the rice and cook for a further 5 minutes, or until lightly golden.

2 **Add the capsicum**, ham, tomatoes, tomato passata, worcestershire and Tabasco sauces and thyme and stir until well combined. Bring mixture to the boil, then reduce heat to low. Cook, covered, for 30–40 minutes, or until rice is tender.

3 **Stir in the parsley** and prawns and season with salt and freshly ground black pepper. Sprinkle with the spring onion, then serve.

SEAFOOD, FENNEL AND POTATO STEW

SERVES 6

| 18–20 black mussels |
| 6 baby octopus |
| 16 raw prawns (shrimp) |
| 1 large fennel bulb |
| 2 tablespoons olive oil |
| 2 leeks, white part only, thinly sliced |
| 2 garlic cloves, crushed |
| ½ teaspoon paprika |
| 2 tablespoons Pernod or Ricard (see Note) |
| 170 ml (5½ fl oz/⅔ cup) dry white wine |
| ¼ teaspoon saffron threads |
| ¼ teaspoon thyme |
| 500 g (1 lb 2 oz) fish cutlets (such as swordfish, kingfish, warehou, monkfish), cut into 6 large chunks |
| 400 g (14 oz) small boiling potatoes or large potatoes, halved |

1 **Scrub the mussels** with a stiff brush and pull out the hairy beards. Discard any broken mussels or open ones that don't close when tapped on the bench. Rinse well.

2 **Use a small**, sharp knife to cut off the octopus heads. Grasp the bodies and push the beaks out with your index finger. Remove and discard. Slit the heads and remove the gut, then wash well.

3 **Peel the prawns**, leaving the tails intact. Gently pull out the dark vein from each prawn back, starting at the head end.

4 **Remove the fennel** fronds and reserve. Trim away any discoloured parts of the fennel and thinly slice. Heat the oil in a large frying pan over medium heat. Add the fennel, leek and garlic. Stir in the paprika, season lightly and cook for 8 minutes, or until softened. Add the Pernod or Ricard and wine and boil for 1 minute, or until reduced by a third.

5 **Add the mussels** to the pan, cover and cook, shaking the pan occasionally for 4–5 minutes, discarding any mussels that haven't opened after that time. Remove from the pan and allow to cool. Remove the mussel meat from the shells and set aside.

6 **Add the saffron** and thyme to the pan and cook, stirring over medium heat, for 1–2 minutes. Season if necessary, then transfer to a large, flameproof casserole dish.

7 **Stir the octopus**, prawns, fish and potatoes into the stew. Cover and cook gently for 10 minutes, or until the potatoes and seafood are tender. Add the mussels, cover and heat through. Garnish with the reserved fennel fronds and serve.

Note: Pernod and Ricard are aniseed-flavoured liqueurs and complement the aniseed taste of the fennel..

MUSHROOM RISOTTO

SERVES 4

1.5 litres (52 fl oz/6 cups) vegetable stock

500 ml (17 fl oz/2 cups) dry white wine

2 tablespoons olive oil

60 g (2 oz) butter

2 leeks, white part only, thinly sliced

1 kg (2 lb 4 oz) flat mushrooms, sliced

500 g (1 lb 2 oz/2¼ cups) arborio rice

75 g (2½ oz/¾ cup) grated parmesan cheese

3 tablespoons chopped flat-leaf (Italian) parsley

balsamic vinegar, to serve

shaved parmesan cheese, to garnish

flat-leaf (Italian) parsley, to garnish

1   Place the stock and wine in a large saucepan, bring to the boil, then reduce the heat to low, cover and keep at a low simmer.

2   Meanwhile, heat the oil and butter in a large saucepan. Add the leek and cook over medium heat for 5 minutes, or until soft and golden. Add the mushrooms to the pan and cook for 5 minutes, or until tender. Add the rice and stir for 1 minute, or until the rice is translucent.

3   Add 125 ml (4 fl oz/½ cup) of hot stock, stirring constantly, over medium heat until the liquid is absorbed. Continue adding more stock, 125 ml (4 fl oz/½ cup) at a time, stirring constantly between additions, for about 25 minutes, or until all the stock is absorbed and the rice is tender and creamy in texture.

4   Stir in the parmesan cheese and chopped parsley and heat for 1 minute, or until the cheese has melted. Serve drizzled with balsamic vinegar and top with parmesan cheese shavings and garnish with the parsley.

CHICKEN AND ASPARAGUS RISOTTO

SERVES 4

1.5 litres (52 fl oz/6 cups) chicken stock

250 ml (9 fl oz/1 cup) dry white wine

6 whole black peppercorns

2 bay leaves

1 tablespoon olive oil

40 g (1½ oz) butter

600 g (1 lb 5 oz) skinless, boneless chicken breasts, cut into 2 cm (¾ inch)cubes

1 leek, sliced

2 garlic cloves, crushed

440 g (15½ oz/2 cups) arborio rice

200 g (7 oz) asparagus, cut into 2.5 cm (1 inch) lengths

50 g (2 oz/½ cup) grated parmesan cheese

2 tablespoons lemon juice

3 tablespoons chopped parsley

shaved parmesan cheese, to garnish

1 Place the stock, wine, peppercorns and bay leaves in a saucepan, and simmer for 5 minutes. Strain, return to the pan and keep at a low simmer.

2 Heat the oil and half the butter in a saucepan, add the chicken and cook over medium heat for 5 minutes, or until golden. Remove. Add leek and garlic and cook for 5 minutes, or until softened.

3 Add the rice and stir for 1 minute to coat. Add 125 ml (4 fl oz/½ cup) stock, stirring until absorbed. Continue adding stock, 125 ml (4 fl oz/½ cup) at a time, stirring constantly for 20–25 minutes, until the stock is absorbed and the rice is tender. Add the asparagus and chicken in the last 5 minutes.

4 When the chicken is cooked through, stir in the parmesan cheese, lemon juice, parsley and remaining butter. Season, and garnish with the shaved parmesan cheese.

CHIVE GNOCCHI WITH BLUE CHEESE

SERVES 4

900 g (2 lb) floury potatoes

330 g (11½ oz/2¼ cups) plain (all-purpose) flour

2 tablespoons chopped chives

4 egg yolks

90 g (3¼ oz) blue cheese

160 ml (5 fl oz/⅔ cup) cream

1 **Peel the potatoes** and cut them into even-sized pieces. Cook them in simmering water for 20 minutes, or until they are tender. Drain them very well, then mash them in a large bowl. Add 280 g (10 oz) of the flour, the chives and egg yolks, along with some seasoning, and mix well. Now add enough of the remaining flour to make a mixture that is soft but not sticky. Divide the mixture into four, roll each bit into a sausage shape 1 cm (½ inch) across and cut off lengths about 1.5 cm (⅝ inch) long. You don't need to shape the gnocchi any more than this.

2 **Bring a large saucepan** of water to the boil and cook the gnocchi in batches. As it rises to the surface (it will do this when it is cooked through), scoop it out with a slotted spoon and drain well.

3 **While the gnocchi** are cooking, put the blue cheese and cream in a saucepan and gently heat them together. Put the gnocchi in a large bowl and pour the blue cheese sauce over it. Gently fold the sauce into the gnocchi and serve.

AROMATIC MEATBALLS IN RICH TOMATO RAGÙ

SERVES 4

3 slices bread, crusts removed

125 ml (4 fl oz/½ cup) milk

4 tablespoons extra virgin olive oil

1 onion, finely chopped

2 garlic cloves, crushed

2 teaspoons chopped thyme

1 tablespoon ground coriander

375 g (13 oz) minced (ground) pork

375 g (13 oz) minced (ground) beef

2 tablespoons grated parmesan cheese,
plus extra to serve

125 ml (4 fl oz/½ cup) dry white wine

400 g (14 oz) tin chopped tomatoes

2 tablespoons sun-dried tomato paste
(concentrated purée)

1 Put the bread slices into a shallow bowl, add the milk and leave to soak for 5 minutes. Crumble up into breadcrumb-sized pieces.

2 Heat half the oil in a frying pan over medium heat and fry the onion, garlic, thyme and 2 teaspoons coriander for 6–8 minutes, or until the onion is softened. Remove from the heat and leave to cool.

3 Mix the combined beef and pork, soaked bread, onion mixture, parmesan, and salt and pepper and, using your hands, work together until evenly combined. Using slightly wet hands, shape the mixture into 24 balls.

4 Heat the remaining oil in a large frying pan and fry the meatballs over a medium heat for 5 minutes, or until browned on all sides. (If the frying pan is small, fry the meatballs in two batches). Add the remaining coriander and cook for 1 minute, or until aromatic.

5 Add wine to the frying pan, bring to the boil and cook for 2 minutes, or until reduced by half. Add tomatoes, sun-dried tomato paste and some pepper and bring to the boil. Cover and cook for 20 minutes, or until meatballs are cooked and the sauce has thickened. Serve with spaghetti and top with parmesan cheese.

CHICKEN AND ALMOND PILAFF

SERVES 4–6

BAHARAT

1½ tablespoons coriander seeds

3 tablespoons black peppercorns

1½ tablespoons cassia bark

1½ tablespoons whole cloves

2 tablespoons cumin seeds

1 teaspoon cardamom seeds

2 whole nutmegs

3 tablespoons paprika

700 g (1 lb 9 oz) boneless, skinless chicken thighs, trimmed and cut into 2.5 cm (1 inch) wide strips

400 g (14 oz/2 cups) basmati rice

750 ml (26 fl oz/3 cups) chicken stock

2 tablespoons ghee

1 large onion, chopped

1 garlic clove, finely chopped

1 teaspoon ground turmeric

400 g (14 oz) tin chopped tomatoes

1 cinnamon stick

4 cardamom pods, bruised

4 whole cloves

½ teaspoon finely grated lemon zest

1 teaspoon salt

3 tablespoons chopped coriander (cilantro) leaves

2 teaspoons lemon juice

4 tablespoons slivered almonds, toasted

1 To make the baharat, grind coriander seeds, peppercorns, cassia bark, cloves, cumin seeds and cardamom seeds to a powder using a mortar and pestle or in a spice grinder—you may need to do this in batches. Grate the nutmeg on the fine side of the grater and add to the spice mixture with the paprika. Stir together.

2 Combine the chicken and 1 tablespoon of the baharat in a large bowl, cover with plastic wrap and refrigerate for 1 hour. Meanwhile, put the rice in a large bowl, cover with cold water and soak for at least 30 minutes. Rinse under cold, running water until the water runs clear, then drain and set aside.

3 Bring the stock to the boil in a saucepan. Reduce the heat, cover and keep at a low simmer. Meanwhile, heat the ghee in a large, heavy-based saucepan over medium heat. Add the onion and garlic and cook for 5 minutes, or until soft and

golden. Add the chicken and turmeric and cook for 5 minutes, or until browned. Add the rice and cook, stirring, for 2 minutes.

4 Add the tomatoes, simmering chicken stock, cinnamon stick, cardamom pods, cloves, lemon zest and salt. Stir well and bring to the boil, then reduce the heat to low and cover the saucepan with a tight-fitting lid. Simmer for 20 minutes, or until the stock is absorbed and the rice is cooked. Remove from the heat and allow to stand, covered, for 10 minutes.

5 Stir in the coriander, lemon juice and almonds. Season.

Note: Baharat keeps well for up to 3 months stored in an airtight jar in a cool, dry place. It can be used in Middle Eastern casseroles and stews, rubbed onto fish that is to be grilled (broiled), pan-fried or barbecued, or used with salt as a spice rub for lamb roasts, cutlets or chops.

ROAST TOMATO RISOTTO

SERVES 4

1 litre (35 fl oz/4 cups) chicken or vegetable stock
pinch of saffron threads
250 ml (9 fl oz/1 cup) dry white wine
2 tablespoons butter
1 onion, finely chopped
270 g (9½ oz/1⅓ cups) risotto rice
1 tablespoon olive oil
1 garlic clove, crushed
400 g (14 oz) cherry tomatoes
4 tablespoons grated parmesan cheese, plus extra, to garnish
4 tablespoons parsley, finely chopped

1   Heat the stock in a saucepan until it is simmering, then leave it over a low heat. Put the saffron into the wine and leave it to soak.

2   Melt the butter in a large, deep heavy-based frying pan, then gently cook the onion until it is soft, but not browned. Add the rice, turn the heat to low and stir well to coat all the grains of rice in the butter.

3   Add the wine and saffron to the rice, turn the heat up to medium and cook, stirring the rice, until all the liquid has been absorbed. Add the hot stock, a couple of ladles at a time, stirring continuously so that the rice cooks evenly and releases some of its starch.

4   While the rice is cooking, heat the oil in a saucepan, add the garlic and tomatoes, then fry for 2–3 minutes over medium heat until the tomatoes are slightly soft and have burst open. Season well.

5   Once all the stock has been added to the rice, taste the rice to see if it is al dente. Stir in the parmesan cheese and the parsley. Spoon the tomatoes over the top and scatter more parmesan cheese on top. Serve straight away.

CHILLI

SERVES 4

165 g (6 oz) dried black beans or kidney beans

3 tablespoons oil

1 red onion, finely chopped

2 garlic cloves, crushed

1½ bunches coriander (cilantro), finely chopped

2 chillies, seeded and finely chopped

1.25 kg (2 lb 12 oz) chuck steak, cut into cubes

600 g (1 lb 5 oz) tinned chopped tomatoes

1½ tablespoons tomato paste (concentrated purée)

375 ml (13 fl oz/1½ cups) beef stock

1½ red capsicums (peppers), seeded and membrane removed, cut into squares

1 large ripe tomato, chopped

1 avocado, diced

2 limes, juiced

4 tablespoons sour cream

1 **Put the beans in a saucepan**, cover with water, bring to the boil, then turn down the heat and simmer for 10 minutes. Turn off the heat and leave for 2 hours. Drain and rinse the beans.

2 **Heat half of the oil** in a large heatproof casserole dish. Cook three-quarters of the onion, garlic, half of the coriander, and the chilli, for 5 minutes.

3 **Remove the onion mixture** from the casserole dish and set aside. Heat half the remaining oil in the dish, add half the steak and cook until well browned. Repeat with the remaining oil and steak. Return the onions and meat to the pan. Add the beans, tinned tomato, tomato paste and stir together. Bring to the boil, then turn it down to a simmer. Put the lid on and cook it for 1 hour 20 minutes. Add the red capsicum to the casserole, stir it in and cook for another 40 minutes.

4 **To make the topping**, mix half of the remaining coriander, the diced tomato, avocado and remaining onion. Season with salt and pepper and add half of the lime juice.

5 **When the meat is tender**, add the remaining coriander and lime juice and season well. Serve with the topping spooned over and a dollop of sour cream.

GREAT TASTES COMFORT FOOD

SAUSAGES COOKED WITH LENTILS

SERVES 4

3 tablespoons olive oil

8 Italian sausages

1 onion, chopped

3 garlic cloves, thinly sliced

2 tablespoons finely chopped rosemary

800 g (1 lb 12 oz) tin tomatoes

16 juniper berries, lightly crushed

1 teaspoon freshly grated nutmeg

1 bay leaf

1 dried chilli

200 ml (7 fl oz) red wine

100 g (3½ oz/½ cup) green lentils

extra rosemary, to garnish

1 Heat olive oil in a large saucepan and cook the sausages for 5–10 minutes, browning well all over. Remove the sausages and set aside.

2 **Reduce the heat to low**, add the onion and garlic to the pan and cook until the onion is soft and translucent, but not browned. Stir in the rosemary, then add the tomatoes and cook gently until the sauce has thickened.

3 **Add the juniper berries**, nutmeg, bay leaf, chilli, red wine and 400 ml (14 fl oz) water. Bring to the boil, then add the lentils and the cooked sausages. Stir well, cover the saucepan and simmer gently for about 40 minutes, or until the lentils are soft. Stir the lentils a few times to prevent them sticking to the base of the pan and add a little more water if you need to cook them for a bit longer. Remove the bay leaf and chilli before serving. Garnish with rosemary.

ROGAN JOSH

SERVES 4–6

1 kg (2 lb 4 oz) boned leg of lamb

1 tablespoon ghee or oil

2 onions, chopped

125 g (4½ oz/½ cup) plain yoghurt

1 teaspoon chilli powder

1 tablespoon ground coriander

2 teaspoons ground cumin

1 teaspoon ground cardamom

½ teaspoon ground cloves

1 teaspoon ground turmeric

3 garlic cloves, crushed

1 tablespoon grated ginger

400 g (14 oz) tin chopped tomatoes

1 teaspoons

3 tablespoons slivered almonds

1 teaspoon garam masala

chopped coriander (cilantro) leaves,
    to garnish

1 Trim the lamb of any excess fat and sinew, and cut it into 2.5 cm (1 inch) cubes.

2 Heat the ghee in a large saucepan, add the onion and cook, stirring, for 5 minutes, or until soft. Stir in the yoghurt, chilli powder, coriander, cumin, cardamom, cloves, turmeric, garlic and ginger. Add the tomato and salt, and simmer for 5 minutes.

3 Add the lamb and stir until coated. Cover and cook over low heat, stirring occasionally, for 1–1½ hours, or until the lamb is tender. Remove the lid and simmer until the liquid thickens.

4 Meanwhile, toast the almonds in a dry frying pan over medium heat for 3–4 minutes, shaking the pan gently, until the nuts are golden brown. Remove from the pan at once to prevent them burning.

5 Add the garam masala to the curry and mix through well. Sprinkle the slivered almonds and coriander leaves over the top and serve.

MUSAMAN BEEF CURRY

SERVES 4

1 tablespoon tamarind pulp (from Asian supermarkets)

2 tablespoons oil

750 g (1 lb 10 oz) lean stewing beef, cubed

500 ml (17 fl oz/2 cups) coconut milk

4 cardamom pods, bruised

500 ml (17 fl oz/2 cups) coconut cream

2–3 tablespoons ready-made Musaman curry paste

2 tablespoons fish sauce

8 baby onions, peeled

8 baby potatoes, peeled

2 tablespoons grated palm sugar or soft brown sugar

80 g (3 oz/½ cup) unsalted peanuts, toasted and ground

1 **Combine the tamarind pulp** and 125 ml (4 fl oz/½ cup) boiling water, and set aside to cool. Mash the pulp with your fingertips to dissolve, then strain, reserving the liquid.

2 **Heat the oil in a wok**. Add beef in batches and cook over high heat for 5 minutes per batch, or until browned. Reduce heat, add the coconut milk and cardamom pods, and simmer for 1 hour, or until the beef is tender. Remove the beef, then strain and reserve the cooking liquid.

3 **Heat the coconut cream** in the wok and stir in the curry paste. Cook for 10 minutes, or until it 'cracks', or the oil separates from the cream. Add the fish sauce, onions, potatoes, beef mixture, palm sugar, peanuts, tamarind water and the reserved liquid. Simmer for 25–30 minutes.

GREEN CHICKEN CURRY

SERVES 4

250 ml (9 fl oz/1 cup) coconut cream

4 tablespoons ready-made green curry paste

8 boneless, skinless chicken thighs or 4 chicken breasts, cut into pieces

250 ml (9 fl oz/1 cup) coconut milk

4 Thai eggplants (aubergines) or ½ of a purple eggplant (aubergine), cut into chunks

2 tablespoons shaved palm sugar (jaggery) or soft brown sugar

2 tablespoons fish sauce

4 makrut (kaffir lime) leaves, torn

1 handful Thai basil leaves

1–2 large red chillies, sliced

coconut milk or cream, for drizzling

1 **Put a wok** over a low heat, add the coconut cream and let it come to the boil. Stir it for a while until the oil separates out. Don't let it burn.

2 **Add the green curry paste**, stir for a minute, then add the chicken. Cook the chicken until it turns opaque, then add the coconut milk and eggplant. Cook for a minute or two until the eggplant is tender. Add the sugar, fish sauce, lime leaves and half of the basil, then mix together.

3 **Garnish with the rest** of the basil, the chilli and a drizzle of coconut milk or cream. Serve with rice.

YELLOW CURRY WITH VEGETABLES

SERVES 4

CURRY PASTE

8 small dried red chillies
1 teaspoon black peppercorns
2 teaspoons coriander seeds
2 teaspoons cumin seeds
1 teaspoon ground turmeric
1½ tablespoons chopped fresh galangal
5 garlic cloves, chopped
1 teaspoon grated ginger
5 red Asian shallots, chopped
2 lemon grass stems, chopped
1 teaspoon shrimp paste
1 teaspoon finely chopped lime zest

2 tablespoons peanut oil
500 ml (17 fl oz/2 cups) coconut cream
125 ml (4 fl oz/½ cup) vegetable stock
150 g (5½ oz) snake (yard-long) beans
150 g (5½ oz) fresh baby corn
1 slender eggplant (aubergine)
100 g cauliflower
2 small zucchini
1 small red capsicum (pepper)
1½ tablespoons fish sauce
1 teaspoon grated palm sugar (jaggery) or soft brown sugar
1 small red chilli, chopped, to garnish
coriander (cilantro) leaves, to garnish

1 To make the curry paste, soak the chillies in boiling water for 15 minutes. Drain and chop. Heat a frying pan, add the peppercorns, coriander seeds, cumin seeds and turmeric, and dry-fry over medium heat for 3 minutes. Transfer to a mortar and pestle or food processor and grind to a fine powder.

2 Place the ground spices, chilli, galangal, garlic, ginger, shallots, lemon grass and shrimp paste in a mortar and pestle and pound until smooth. Stir in the lime zest.

3 Cut the eggplant, capsicum and zucchini into 1 cm (½ in) slices. Cut the snake beans into 2.5 cm (1 inch) lengths. Cut the cauliflower into small florets. Set aside.

4 Heat a wok over medium heat, add the oil and swirl to coat. Add 2 tablespoons of curry paste and cook for 1 minute. Add 250 ml (9 fl oz/1 cup) of coconut cream and cook over medium heat for 10 minutes, or until the mixture is thick and the oil separates.

5 Add the stock, vegetables and remaining coconut cream and cook for 5 minutes, or until the vegetables are tender, but still crisp. Stir in the fish sauce and sugar and garnish with the chilli and coriander.

MADRAS BEEF CURRY

SERVES 4

1 tablespoon oil or ghee

1 onion, chopped

3–4 tablespoons ready-made Madras
curry paste

1 kg (2 lb 4 oz) skirt or chuck steak,
trimmed and cut into 2.5 cm (1 inch)
cubes

3 tablespoons tomato paste
(concentrated purée)

250 ml (9 fl oz/1 cup) beef stock

1 Heat the oil in a large frying pan, add the onion and cook over medium heat for 10 minutes, or until browned. Add the curry paste and stir for 1 minute, or until fragrant.

2 Add the meat and cook, stirring, until coated with the curry paste.

3 Stir in the tomato paste and beef stock. Reduce the heat and simmer, covered, for 1 hour 15 minutes, and then uncovered for 15 minutes, or until the meat is tender.

BURMESE CHICKEN CURRY

SERVES 4–6

1 tablespoon medium spiced Indian curry powder

1 teaspoon garam masala

½ teaspoon cayenne pepper

2 teaspoons sweet paprika

1.6 kg (3 lb 8 oz) chicken, cut into 8 pieces or 1.6 kg (3 lb 8 oz) mixed chicken pieces

2 onions, chopped

3 garlic cloves, crushed

2 teaspoons grated ginger

2 tomatoes, chopped

2 teaspoons tomato paste (concentrated purée)

1 lemon grass stem, white part only, thinly sliced

3 tablespoons oil

500 ml (17 fl oz/2 cups) chicken stock

½ teaspoon sugar

1 tablespoon fish sauce

1 **Mix the curry** powder, garam masala, cayenne pepper and paprika in a bowl. Rub this spice mix all over the chicken pieces and set aside.

2 **Put the onions**, garlic, ginger, tomatoes, tomato paste and lemon grass in a food processor, or in a mortar with a pestle, and process or pound to a smooth paste.

3 **In a large** heavy-based frying pan (that will fit the chicken pieces in a single layer), heat oil over medium heat, add the chicken and brown all over, then remove from the pan. In the same frying pan, add the onion paste, and cook over low heat for 5–8 minutes stirring constantly. Put the chicken back into the pan, and turn to coat in the paste.

4 **Add the chicken** stock and sugar and bring to a simmer. Reduce heat to low, cover and cook for 1¼ hours, or until the chicken is very tender. While cooking, skim any oil that comes to the surface and discard. Stir in the fish sauce and serve.

GOAN PORK CURRY

SERVES 6

2 teaspoons cumin seeds

2 teaspoons black mustard seeds

1 teaspoon cardamom seeds

1 teaspoon ground turmeric

1 teaspoon ground cinnamon

½ teaspoon black peppercorns

6 whole cloves

5 small dried red chillies

4 tablespoons white vinegar

1 tablespoon soft brown sugar

1 teaspoon salt

4 tablespoons oil

1 large onion, chopped

6–8 garlic cloves, crushed

1 tablespoon finely grated ginger

1.5 kg (3 lb 5 oz) pork leg, cut into 3 cm (1 inch) cubes

1 Dry-fry the spices and chillies in a large frying pan for 2 minutes, or until fragrant. Place in a spice grinder or food processor and grind until finely ground. Transfer to a bowl and stir in the vinegar, sugar and salt to form a paste.

2 Heat half the oil in a large saucepan. Add the chopped onion and cook for 5 minutes, or until lightly golden. Place the onion in a food processor with 2 tablespoons cold water and process until smooth. Stir into the spice paste.

3 Place the garlic and ginger in a small bowl, mix together well and stir in 2 tablespoons water.

4 Heat remaining oil in the pan over high heat. Add the cubed pork and cook in 3–4 batches for 8 minutes, or until well browned. Return all the meat to the pan and stir in the garlic and ginger mixture. Add the onion mixture and 250 ml (9 fl oz/1 cup) hot water. Simmer, covered, for 1 hour, or until the pork is tender. Uncover, bring to the boil and cook, stirring frequently, for 10 minutes, or until the sauce reduces and thickens slightly. Serve with rice and poppadoms.

MALAYSIAN NONYA CHICKEN CURRY

SERVES 4

CURRY PASTE

2 red onions, chopped

4 small red chillies, seeded and sliced

4 garlic cloves, sliced

2 lemon grass stems, white part only, sliced

3 cm x 2 cm (1¼ inch x ¾ inch) piece galangal or ginger, sliced

8 makrut (kaffir lime) leaves, roughly chopped

1 teaspoon ground turmeric

½ teaspoon shrimp paste, dry-roasted

2 tablespoons oil

750 g (1 lb 10 oz) chicken thigh fillets, cut into bite-size pieces

400 ml (14 fl oz) coconut milk

3 tablespoons tamarind purée

1 tablespoon fish sauce

3 makrut (kaffir lime) leaves, shredded

1 To make the curry paste, place all of the ingredients in a food processor or blender and process to a thick paste.

2 Heat a wok or large saucepan over high heat, add the oil and swirl to coat the side. Add the curry paste and cook, stirring occasionally, over low heat for 8–10 minutes, or until fragrant. Add the chicken and stir-fry with the paste for 2–3 minutes.

3 Add the coconut milk, tamarind purée and fish sauce to the wok, and simmer, stirring occasionally, for 15–20 minutes, or until the chicken is tender. Garnish with the lime leaves. Serve with rice and steamed bok choy (pak choy).

BEEF RENDANG

SERVES 4

1 kg (2 lb 4 oz) topside beef, cut into 1 cm (½ inch) thick strips

2 onions, chopped

1 tablespoon chopped fresh ginger

3 garlic cloves, finely chopped

1 teaspoon ground turmeric

2 teaspoons ground coriander

2½ tablespoons sambal oelek

100 ml (3½ oz) oil

400 ml (14 fl oz) coconut cream

6 curry leaves

1 lemon grass stem, white part only, bruised

100 ml (3½ fl oz) tamarind purée

4 makrut (kaffir lime) leaves

1 teaspoon soft brown sugar

1 makrut (kaffir lime) leaf, extra, shredded, to garnish

1 Season the beef with salt and white pepper. Place the onion, ginger, garlic, turmeric, coriander and sambal oelek in a blender, and blend until smooth. Add a little water, if needed.

2 Heat the oil in a large saucepan, add the spice paste and cook over medium heat for 5 minutes, or until fragrant. Add the beef, stir to coat in the spices and cook for 1–2 minutes. Add the coconut cream, curry leaves, lemon grass, tamarind purée, lime leaves and 500 ml (17 fl oz/2 cups) water. Reduce the heat and simmer over low heat for 2½ hours, or until the meat is tender and the sauce has thickened. Add a little water, if necessary, to prevent the sauce sticking. Stir in the sugar. Garnish with the shredded makrut leaf and serve with rice.

LAMB KORMA

SERVES 4–6

2 tablespoons blanched almonds

2 teaspoons grated ginger

4 garlic cloves, crushed

½ teaspoon ground cinnamon

½ teaspoon ground cardamom

¼ teaspoon ground cloves

½ teaspoon chilli powder

½ teaspoon ground mace

1½ teaspoons paprika

1 teaspoon ground coriander

4 tablespoons ghee

2 onions, thinly sliced

1 kg (2 lb 4 oz) boned leg of lamb, cubed

¼ teaspoon saffron threads, soaked in 1 tablespoon warm water

250 g (9 fl oz/1 cup) plain yoghurt

125 g (4½ oz/½ cup) sour cream

coriander (cilantro) sprigs, to garnish

1 **Place the almonds,** ginger and garlic in a blender with 3 tablespoons water. Blend until smooth. Add ground spices, and blend for 10 seconds, or until combined.

2 **Heat ghee** in a casserole dish, add onion and cook over medium heat for 10–15 minutes, or until caramelized. Add the spice paste and cook, stirring to prevent sticking, for 5 minutes, or until fragrant.

3 **Add the meat** and toss to coat in the spices. Cook, stirring, for 5 minutes, or until browned.

4 **Add the saffron** and soaking liquid, half the yoghurt and half the sour cream. Season with salt and bring to the boil, then reduce the heat and simmer, covered, for 2 hours, or until the meat is tender. Stir frequently to prevent sticking, as the curry is quite dry when cooked. Skim any fat from the surface. Stir in the remaining yoghurt and sour cream, and garnish with the coriander. Serve with rice.

VEGETABLE CASSEROLE

SERVES 6–8

TOMATO SAUCE

1 kg (2 lb 4 oz) tomatoes

2 tablespoons olive oil

3 garlic cloves, crushed

1 red onion, finely chopped

2 teaspoons thyme, chopped

250 ml (9 fl oz/1 cup) olive oil

500 g (1 lb 2 oz) all-purpose potatoes, cut into 5 mm (¼ in) rounds

500 g (1 lb 2 oz) eggplant (aubergine), cut into 5 mm (¼ inch) rounds

500 g (1 lb 2 oz) green capsicum (pepper), seeded and membrane removed, cut into 2.5 cm (1 inch) pieces

1 large handful flat-leaf (Italian) parsley, roughly chopped

1 **To make the tomato sauce**, score a cross in the base of each tomato. Put in a heatproof bowl and cover with boiling water. Leave for 30 seconds, then transfer to cold water and peel the skin away from the cross. Cut each tomato in half, scoop out the seeds and finely chop the flesh. Heat the oil in a heavy-based frying pan and cook the garlic and onion over low heat for 5–6 minutes, or until softened. Add the tomato and thyme and cook for 20 minutes over medium heat, or until thickened. Season to taste.

2 **While the sauce is cooking**, heat the oil in a heavy-based frying pan over low heat and cook the potato in batches until tender but not brown. Remove with a slotted spoon or tongs and place in a casserole dish measuring about 5 x 21 x 27 cm (2 x 8¼ x 10¾ inches). Lightly season.

3 **Increase the heat** to high and pan-fry the eggplant for 15 minutes, or until golden, turning after about 7 minutes. Drain the slices on paper towels, then place on top of the potatoes. Season lightly. Preheat oven to 180°C (350°F/Gas 4).

4 **Cook the capsicum** in the same pan until tender but not browned, adding a little more olive oil if needed. Remove with a slotted spoon, drain on paper towels and arrange over the eggplant. Season lightly. Pour the tomato sauce over the top and bake for 20 minutes. Serve warm, sprinkled with parsley.

PORK VINDALOO

SERVES 4

1 kg (2 lb 4 oz) diced pork

3 tablespoons white vinegar

2.5 cm (1 inch) piece ginger, peeled, finely grated

5 garlic cloves, crushed

½ teaspoon ground black pepper

1 teaspoon salt

1 tablespoon ground fenugreek

2 teaspoons ground cumin

1 teaspoon ground cinnamon

1 teaspoon chilli flakes

½ teaspoon ground cardamom

2 tablespoons ghee

1 onion, chopped

750 ml (26 fl oz/3 cups) beef stock

1 teaspoon cornflour (cornstarch)

20 g (¾ oz) palm sugar (jaggery) or soft brown sugar

cooked basmati rice, to serve

1 **Combine the pork**, vinegar, ginger, garlic, pepper, salt and spices in a large bowl and mix well. Cover and refrigerate for 2 hours, or overnight.

2 **Heat ghee** in a large saucepan over medium heat and cook the pork in batches until lightly browned. Add the onion to the same pan and cook, stirring, for about 3 minutes, or until soft. Return the pork to the pan with the stock, and bring to the boil. Season to taste with salt. Reduce the heat to low and cook, covered, for 1½ hours, or until the pork is tender.

3 **Combine the cornflour** and 1 teaspoon of water in a small jug and add to the pork mixture. Bring to the boil over high heat until the mixture thickens slightly. Stir in the palm sugar until dissolved. Serve the pork vindaloo with basmati rice.

PANANG BEEF

SERVES 4–6

CURRY PASTE

8–10 large dried red chillies

6 red Asian shallots, chopped

6 garlic cloves, chopped

1 teaspoon ground coriander

1 tablespoon ground cumin

1 teaspoon white pepper

2 lemon grass stems, white part only, bruised and sliced

1 tablespoon chopped galangal or ginger

6 coriander (cilantro) roots

2 teaspoons shrimp paste

2 tablespoons peanuts, toasted

400 ml (14 fl oz) tinned coconut cream (do not shake)

1 kg (2 lb 4 oz) round or blade steak, cut into 1 cm (½ in) slices

400 ml (14 fl oz) tin coconut milk

4 tablespoons crunchy peanut butter

4 makrut (kaffir lime) leaves

3 tablespoons lime juice

2½ tablespoons fish sauce

3–4 tablespoons grated palm sugar (jaggery) or soft brown sugar

chopped toasted peanuts, to garnish

Thai basil, to garnish

1 To make the curry paste, put the chillies in a bowl and cover with boiling water. Soak for 20 minutes, or until softened. Remove the seeds and roughly chop the flesh. Put the chopped chillies in a food processor along with the shallots, garlic, ground coriander, ground cumin, white pepper, lemon grass, galangal, coriander roots, shrimp paste and toasted peanuts and process until a smooth paste forms. You might need to add a little water if the paste is too thick.

2 Open the tin of coconut cream and scoop off the really thick cream from the top. Put this thick cream in a wok and cook over medium heat for 10 minutes, or until the oil starts to separate from the cream. Stir in 8 tablespoons of the curry paste and cook, stirring often, for 5–8 minutes, or until fragrant. Add the beef, coconut milk, peanut butter, makrut leaves and the remaining coconut cream to the wok and cook for 8 minutes, or until the beef just starts to change colour. Reduce the heat to low and simmer for 30 minutes, or until the beef is tender, stirring every few minutes to prevent it from catching on the bottom. Stir in the lime juice, fish sauce and sugar until they are mixed into the curry. Serve with steamed rice and garnish with the roasted peanuts and basil.

BALTI LAMB

SERVES 4

1 kg (2 lb 4 oz) lamb leg steaks,
    cut into 2.5 cm (1 inch) cubes

5 tablespoons ready-made Balti curry
    paste

2 tablespoons ghee or vegetable oil

1 large onion, finely chopped

3 garlic cloves, crushed

1 tablespoon garam masala

2 tablespoons chopped coriander
    (cilantro) leaves, plus extra, to garnish

poppadoms, to serve

steamed rice, to serve

1 **Put the lamb**, 1 tablespoon of the curry paste and 1 litre (35 fl oz/4 cups) boiling water in a wok and mix together. Bring to the boil over high heat then reduce the heat to very low and cook, covered, for 40–50 minutes, or until the meat is almost cooked through. Drain, set the meat aside, and reserve the sauce.

2 **Heat the ghee** in a clean wok over medium heat. Add the onion and cook for 5–7 minutes, or until soft. Add the garlic and garam masala and cook for a further 2–3 minutes. Increase the heat, add the remaining curry paste and return the lamb to the wok. Cook for 5 minutes, or until the meat has browned. Slowly add the reserved sauce and simmer over low heat, stirring occasionally, for 15 minutes. Add the chopped coriander leaves and 250 ml (9 fl oz/1 cup) water and simmer for 15 minutes, or until the meat is tender and the sauce has thickened slightly. Season to taste.

3 **Garnish with the extra** coriander leaves and serve with poppadoms and steamed rice.

LAMB KOFTAS IN SPICY TOMATO SAUCE

SERVES 4

3 tablespoons oil

2 large onions, finely chopped

3 garlic cloves, finely chopped

1½ tablespoons garam masala

½ teaspoon chilli powder

400 g (14 oz) tin chopped tomatoes

1 tablespoon tomato paste
   (concentrated purée)

500 ml (17 fl oz/2 cups) beef stock

270 ml (9½ fl oz) tin coconut milk

500 g (1 lb 2 oz) minced (ground) lamb

1 large handful mint, finely chopped,
   plus extra, to garnish

1 large handful coriander (cilantro)
   leaves, finely chopped, plus extra,
   to garnish

1 egg, lightly beaten

juice of 1 lime

steamed basmati rice, to serve

1 Heat the oil in a large heavy-based frying pan. Cook the onion for 5 minutes, or until lightly brown. Add garlic, garam masala and chilli powder. Cook, stirring for 2–3 minutes, or until aromatic. Remove half of the onion mixture to a large bowl and set aside to cool.

2 Add the chopped tomatoes and tomato paste to the remaining onion in the frying pan, stirring. Simmer 5 minutes, then add the stock and coconut milk. Bring to the boil, then remove from the heat, cover and set aside.

3 Add the lamb, herbs and beaten egg to the cooled onion mixture. With clean wet hands, roll the meat into 28 walnut-sized balls. Cover and refrigerate for 30 minutes to allow the flavours to develop.

4 Heat the sauce to simmering point. Add the kofta balls and cook over low heat for 1 hour, or until cooked through and the sauce has reduced and thickened. Gently stir the kofta balls occasionally. Stir in the lime juice. Garnish with the extra herbs and serve with basmati rice.

CHICKEN IN GARLIC SAUCE

SERVES 6

1 kg (2 lb 4 oz) boneless, skinless chicken thighs
1 tablespoon sweet paprika
2 tablespoons olive oil
8 garlic cloves, unpeeled
3 tablespoons dry sherry
125 ml (4 fl oz/½ cup) chicken stock
1 bay leaf
2 tablespoons chopped flat-leaf (Italian) parsley

1 Trim any excess fat from the chicken and cut the thighs into thirds. Combine the paprika with some salt and pepper in a bowl, add the chicken and toss to coat.

2 Heat half the oil in a large frying pan over high heat and cook the garlic cloves for 1–2 minutes, or until brown. Remove from pan. Cook the chicken in batches for 5 minutes, or until brown all over. Return all the chicken to the pan, add sherry, boil for 30 seconds, then add stock and bay leaf. Reduce heat and simmer, covered, over low heat for 10 minutes.

3 Meanwhile, squeeze the garlic pulp from their skins and pound with the parsley into a paste using a mortar and pestle or a small bowl and the back of a spoon. Stir into the chicken, then cover and cook for 10 minutes, or until tender. Serve hot.

MOROCCAN VEGETABLE STEW WITH MINTY COUSCOUS

SERVES 4

2 tablespoons olive oil

1 onion, finely chopped

3 garlic cloves, finely chopped

1 teaspoon ground ginger

1 teaspoon ground turmeric

2 teaspoons ground cumin

2 teaspoons ground cinnamon

½ teaspoon chilli flakes

400 g (14 oz) tin diced tomatoes

400 g (14 oz) tin chickpeas, rinsed and drained

60 g (2 oz/½ cup) sultanas (golden raisins)

400 g (14 oz) butternut pumpkin (squash), peeled and cut into 3 cm (1 inch) cubes

2 large zucchini (250 g/9 oz), cut into 2 cm (¾ inch) pieces

2 carrots, cut into 2 cm (¾ inch) pieces

185 g (6½ oz/1 cup) instant couscous

2 tablespoons butter

4 tablespoons chopped mint

1 Heat the olive oil in a large saucepan over medium heat. Add onion and cook for 3–5 minutes, or until translucent but not brown. Add garlic, ginger, turmeric, cumin, cinnamon and chilli flakes. Cook for 1 minute. Add tomato, chickpeas, sultanas and 250 ml (9 fl oz/1 cup) water. Bring to the boil, reduce the heat and simmer, covered, for 20 minutes. Add pumpkin, zucchini and carrot, and cook for a further 20 minutes, or until the vegetables are tender. Season with salt and black pepper.

2 Place the couscous in a large, heatproof bowl. Cover with 250 ml (9 fl oz/1 cup) boiling water and leave to stand for 5 minutes, or until all the water is absorbed. Fluff with a fork and stir in the butter and mint. Season with salt and ground black pepper, and serve with the stew.

LAMB TAGINE

SERVES 4

1 tablespoon ground cumin

1 teaspoon ground ginger

½ teaspoon ground turmeric

1 teaspoon paprika

½ teaspoon ground cinnamon

2 garlic cloves, crushed

4 tablespoons olive oil

1 teaspoon salt

1.5 kg (3 lb 5 oz) diced lamb shoulder

2 onions, sliced

500 ml (17 fl oz/2 cups) beef stock

2 tomatoes, peeled and chopped

½ teaspoon saffron threads

1 carrot, cut into matchsticks

1 large handful chopped coriander (cilantro) leaves

155 g (5½ oz/1 cup) pitted kalamata olives

1 teaspoon finely chopped rinsed preserved lemon zest (see Note)

370 g (13 oz/2 cups) instant couscous

60 g (2 oz) butter

1½ tablespoons honey

1 Place the cumin, ginger, turmeric, paprika, cinnamon, crushed garlic, 2 tablespoons oil and the salt in a large bowl. Mix together, add the lamb and toss to coat. Refrigerate for 2 hours.

2 Heat the remaining oil in a large casserole dish over medium heat, add the lamb in batches and cook for 5–6 minutes, or until browned. Return the meat to the dish, add the onion and cook for 1–2 minutes. Add the stock, tomato, saffron, carrot and coriander. Bring to the boil, then reduce the heat to low and cook, covered, for 1 hour. Add the olives and preserved lemon and cook, uncovered, for 30 minutes.

3 Place couscous in a large heatproof bowl. Add 375 ml (13 fl oz/1½ cups) boiling water and leave to stand for about 5 minutes. Stir in the butter and fluff up with a fork. Season. Spoon into deep bowls, top with the tagine and drizzle with the honey.

Note: Preserved lemons are much used in Moroccan cookery and are available in jars from delicatessens and some supermarkets. Only use the rinsed zest of preserved lemons. Discard the bitter pith and flesh.

GREEK OCTOPUS IN RED WINE STEW

SERVES 4–6

1 kg (2 lb 4 oz) baby octopus

2 tablespoons olive oil

1 large onion, chopped

3 garlic cloves, crushed

1 bay leaf

750 ml (26 fl oz/3 cups) red wine

3 tablespoons red wine vinegar

400 g (14 oz) tin crushed tomatoes

1 tablespoon tomato paste
    (concentrated purée)

1 tablespoon chopped oregano

¼ teaspoon ground cinnamon

small pinch of ground cloves

1 teaspoon sugar

2 tablespoons finely chopped flat-leaf
    (Italian) parsley

1 Cut between the head and tentacles of the octopus, just below the eyes. Grasp the body and push the beak out and up through the centre of the tentacles with your fingers. Cut the eyes from the head by slicing a small round off. Discard the eye section. Carefully slit through one side, avoiding the ink sac, and remove any gut from inside. Rinse the octopus well under running water.

2 Heat oil in a large saucepan, add the onion and cook over a medium heat for 5 minutes, or until starting to brown. Add the garlic and bay leaf, and cook for 1 minute further. Add the octopus and stir to coat in the onion mixture.

3 Stir in the wine, vinegar, tomato, tomato paste, oregano, cinnamon, cloves and sugar. Bring to the boil, then reduce the heat and simmer for 1 hour, or until the octopus is tender and the sauce has thickened slightly. Stir in the parsley and season to taste with salt and ground black pepper. Serve with a Greek salad and crusty bread to mop up the delicious juices.

SERVES 6–8

300 g (10½ oz) red mullet fillets

400 g (14 oz) firm white fish fillets

300 g (10½ oz) cleaned calamari

1.5 litres (52 fl oz/6 cups) fish stock

4 tablespoons olive oil

1 onion, chopped

6 garlic cloves, chopped

1 small red chilli, chopped

1 teaspoon paprika

pinch of saffron threads

150 ml (5 fl oz) dry white wine

400 g (14 oz) tin crushed tomatoes

16 raw medium prawns (shrimp), peeled, deveined, tails intact

2 tablespoons brandy

24 black mussels, cleaned

1 tablespoon chopped parsley

PICADA

2 tablespoons olive oil

2 slices day-old bread, cubed

2 garlic cloves

5 blanched almonds, toasted

2 tablespoons flat-leaf (Italian) parsley

1 Cut fish and calamari into 4 cm (1½ inch) pieces. Place the stock in a large saucepan and bring to the boil for 15 minutes, or until reduced by half.

2 To make the picada, heat the oil in a frying pan and cook the bread, stirring, for 2 minutes, or until golden, adding the garlic for the last minute. Place all of the ingredients in a food processor and process, adding stock to make a smooth paste.

3 Heat 2 tablespoons of the oil in a saucepan, add the onion, garlic, chilli and paprika, and cook, stirring, for 1 minute. Add the saffron, wine, tomatoes and stock. Bring to the boil, reduce the heat and simmer. Heat the remaining oil in a frying pan and fry fish and calamari for 3–5 minutes. Remove from the pan. Add prawns, cook for 1 minute, pour in the brandy. Carefully ignite the brandy and let the flames burn down. Remove from the pan.

4 Add the mussels to the pan and simmer, covered, for 2–3 minutes, or until opened. Discard any that do not open. Add all the seafood and the picada to the pan, stirring until the sauce has thickened and the seafood is cooked. Season, sprinkle with the parsley and serve.

MEDITERRANEAN CHICKEN STEW

SERVES 4–6

1 teaspoon ground cumin

1 teaspoon ground coriander

1 teaspoon paprika

¼ teaspoon ground ginger

1.5 kg (3 lb 5 oz) boneless, skinless chicken thighs, quartered

2 tablespoons olive oil

1 large onion, sliced

3 garlic cloves, finely chopped

2 teaspoons oregano, chopped

250 ml (9 fl oz/1 cup) dry white wine

420 g (15 oz) can crushed tomatoes

300 ml (10½ fl oz) chicken stock

2 bay leaves, crushed

¼ teaspoon saffron threads, soaked in 2 tablespoons warm water

3 tablespoons good-quality pitted green olives

½ preserved lemon, flesh removed and zest cut into fine slivers

3 tablespoons finely chopped flat-leaf (Italian) parsley

basil sprigs, to garnish

1 **Combine the cumin,** coriander, paprika and ginger, and rub over the chicken pieces.

2 **Heat the oil** in a large saucepan. Add the chicken in batches and cook over medium heat for 5 minutes, or until browned. Remove from the pan.

3 **Reduce the heat,** add onion and cook, stirring constantly, for 5 minutes, or until golden. Add the garlic and oregano, and cook for 2 minutes, then add the wine and cook for 6 minutes, or until nearly evaporated. Add tomato, stock, bay leaves and saffron and soaking liquid, and bring to the boil. Return chicken to the pan and season well. Reduce heat and simmer, covered, for 30 minutes, or until chicken is cooked through.

4 **Stir in the olives** and preserved lemon. Cook, uncovered, for 10 minutes. Stir in the parsley and garnish with the sprigs of basil just before serving.

Note: This stew is delicious served with mashed potato. For extra flavour, stir some shredded fresh basil through the potato before serving.

CHICKEN CACCIATORA

SERVES 4

3 tablespoons olive oil

1 large onion, finely chopped

3 garlic cloves, crushed

150 g (5½ oz) pancetta, finely chopped

125 g (4½ oz) button mushrooms, thickly sliced

1 large chicken (at least 1.6 kg/3 lb 8 oz), cut into 8 pieces

4 tablespoons dry vermouth or dry white wine

800 g (1 lb 12 oz) tinned chopped tomatoes

¼ teaspoon soft brown sugar

¼ teaspoon cayenne pepper

1 oregano sprig

1 thyme sprig

1 bay leaf

1 Heat half the olive oil in a large flameproof casserole dish. Add the onion and garlic and cook for 6–8 minutes over low heat, stirring, until the onion is golden. Add the pancetta and mushrooms, increase the heat and cook, stirring, for 4–5 minutes. Transfer to a bowl.

2 Add the remaining oil to the casserole dish and brown the chicken pieces, a few at a time, over medium heat. Season as they brown. Spoon off the excess fat and return the chicken to the casserole dish. Increase the heat, add the vermouth and cook until the liquid hascalmost evaporated.

3 Add the chopped tomato, brown sugar, cayenne pepper, oregano, thyme and bay leaf, and stir in 4 tablespoons water. Bring to the boil, then stir in reserved onion mixture. Reduce the heat, cover and simmer for 25 minutes, or until the chicken is tender but not falling off the bone.

4 If the liquid is too thin, remove chicken from the casserole dish, increase the heat and boil until the liquid has thickened. Discard the sprigs of herbs and adjust the seasoning.

BEAN AND CAPSICUM STEW

SERVES 4–6

200 g (7 oz/1 cup) dried haricot beans
  (see Note)

2 tablespoons olive oil

2 large garlic cloves, crushed

1 red onion, halved and cut into thin
  wedges

1 red capsicum (pepper), cut into 1.5 cm
  (½ inch) cubes

1 green capsicum (pepper), cut into
  1.5 cm (½ inch) cubes

2 x 400 g (14 oz) tins chopped tomatoes

2 tablespoons tomato paste
  (concentrated purée)

500 ml (17 fl oz/2 cups) vegetable stock

2 tablespoons chopped basil

125 g (4½ oz/⅔ cup) Kalamata olives,
  pitted

1–2 teaspoons soft brown sugar

1 Put the beans in a large bowl, cover with cold water and soak overnight. Rinse well, then transfer to a large saucepan, cover with cold water and cook for 45 minutes, or until just tender. Drain.

2 Heat the oil in a large saucepan. Cook the garlic and onion over medium heat for 2–3 minutes, or until the onion is soft. Add the red and green capsicum and cook for a further 5 minutes.

3 Stir in tomato, tomato paste, stock and beans. Simmer, covered, for 40 minutes, or until the beans are cooked through. Stir in the basil, olives and sugar. Season with salt and black pepper. Serve hot with crusty bread.

Note: 200 g (1 cup) dried haricot beans yields about 500 g (2½ cups) cooked beans. You can use 2½ cups tinned haricot or borlotti (cranberry) beans instead if you prefer.

SPICY SAUSAGE STEW

SERVES 4

2 tablespoons olive oil

8 Italian sausages (700 g/1 lb 9 oz), cut into 4 cm (1½ inch) lengths

1 leek, white part removed, finely sliced

1 red capsicum (pepper), seeded and chopped

425 g (15 oz) tin chopped tomatoes

125 ml (4 fl oz/½ cup) chicken stock

300 g (10½ oz) tin butterbeans (lima beans), rinsed and drained

250 g (9 oz/1⅓ cups) instant couscous

2 tablespoons butter, melted

2 tablespoons flat-leaf (Italian) parsley

1 **Heat half the oil** in a saucepan over medium heat, add the sausage and cook for 6 minutes, or until browned. Remove from pan. Cook the sliced leek in the remaining oil over low heat for 10–12 minutes, or until soft. Add capsicum and cook for 1–2 minutes. Return the sausage to the pan and stir in the tomato and stock. Bring to the boil, then reduce the heat and simmer for 30 minutes. Add the beans, season and stir for 1–2 minutes to heat through.

2 **Place the couscous** in a heatproof bowl with 330 ml (11 fl oz/1⅓ cups) boiling water and a pinch of salt. Leave for 5 minutes, fluff up and stir in the butter. Divide among four bowls and spoon on the stew. Garnish with the parsley.

ASIAN-FLAVOURED BEEF STEW

SERVES 4

2 tablespoons olive oil

1 kg (2 lb 4 oz) chuck steak, cut into
   2.5 cm (1 inch) cubes

1 large red onion, thickly sliced

3 garlic cloves, crushed

3 tablespoons tomato paste

250 ml (9 fl oz/1 cup) red wine

500 ml (17 fl oz/2 cups) beef stock

2 bay leaves, crushed

3 x 1.5 cm (½ inch) strips orange zest

1 star anise

1 teaspoon sichuan peppercorns

1 teaspoon chopped thyme

1 tablespoon chopped rosemary

3 tablespoons chopped coriander
   (cilantro) leaves

1 **Heat 1 tablespoon oil** in a large saucepan, add the beef and cook in batches over medium heat for 2 minutes, or until browned. Remove.

2 **Heat the remaining oil**, add the onion and garlic and cook for 5 minutes. Add the tomato paste, cook for 3 minutes, then stir in the wine and cook for 2 minutes.

3 **Return the meat** to the pan and add stock, bay leaves, orange zest, star anise, sichuan peppercorns, thyme and rosemary. Reduce the heat to low and simmer, covered, for 1½ hours–2 hours, or until tender. Remove the bay leaves and zest. Stir in 2½ tablespoons coriander and garnish with the remainder. Serve with rice.

HOISIN BEEF STEW

SERVES 6

1½ tablespoons oil
1 kg (2 lb 4 oz) chuck beef steak, cut into 3 cm (1¼ in) cubes
1 tablespoon finely chopped ginger
1 tablespoon finely chopped garlic
1 litre (35 fl oz/4 cups) beef stock
4 tablespoons Chinese rice wine
4 tablespoons hoisin sauce
5 cm (2 inch) piece cassia bark
1 piece dried tangerine peel
2 star anise
1 teaspoon sichuan peppercorns, lightly crushed
2 teaspoons soft brown sugar
300 g (10½ oz) daikon, cut into 2.5 cm (1 inch) chunks
3 spring onions (scallions), cut into 2.5 cm (1 inch) lengths, plus extra, to garnish
50 g (2 oz) tinned bamboo shoots, sliced
a few drops sesame oil (optional)
steamed rice, to serve

1 **Heat a wok** until very hot, add the oil and swirl to coat the base and side. Stir-fry the beef in batches for 1–2 minutes, or until browned all over. Remove from the wok and set aside.

2 **Add the ginger** and garlic to the wok and stir-fry for a few seconds. Add the stock, rice wine, hoisin sauce, cassia bark, tangerine peel, star anise, sichuan peppercorns, sugar, daikon and 875 ml (30 fl oz/3½ cups) water then return the beef to the wok.

3 **Bring to the boil**, skimming any scum that forms on the surface, then reduce to a simmer and cook, stirring occasionally for 1½ hours, or until the beef is tender and the sauce has thickened slightly. Add the spring onion and the bamboo shoots 5 minutes before the end of the cooking time. Stir in a few drops of sesame oil and garnish with extra spring onion, if desired. Serve with steamed rice.

Note: You can remove the star anise, cassia bark and tangerine peel before serving or leave them in the serving dish for presentation.

BEEF BOURGUIGNON

SERVES 6

1 kg (2 lb 4 oz) chuck steak, cut into
    3 cm (1¼ inch) cubes

seasoned flour, to coat

2 tablespoons oil

200 g (7 oz) bacon, chopped

2 tablespoons butter

150 g (5½ oz) baby onions

3 garlic cloves, finely chopped

1 leek, white part removed, sliced

250 g (9 oz) button mushrooms

2 carrots, diced

3 tablespoons tomato paste

500 ml (17 fl oz/2 cups) red wine

500 ml (17 fl oz/2 cups) beef stock

2 teaspoons chopped thyme

2 bay leaves

4 tablespoons finely chopped flat-leaf
    (Italian) parsley

1 Toss the meat in the flour to coat. Shake off any excess. Heat the oil in a large saucepan, add the bacon and cook over medium heat for 3–4 minutes, or until lightly browned. Remove from the pan. Add beef in small batches and cook for 3–4 minutes, or until starting to brown. Remove from pan.

2 Melt the butter in the pan, add the onions, garlic and leek, and cook for 4–5 minutes, or until softened.

3 Return the beef and bacon to the pan, add the remaining ingredients, except the parsley, and stir well. Bring to the boil, reduce the heat and simmer, covered, stirring occasionally, for 1 hour, then uncovered for 30 minutes, or until the meat is very tender and the sauce thickened. Remove the bay leaves and stir in the parsley. Serve with mashed potato.

SERVES 6

100 g (3½ oz) bacon, cut into thin

1 onion, chopped

2 tomatoes, peeled and chopped

1 garlic clove, chopped

½ teaspoon caraway seeds, lightly crushed

1½ tablespoons sweet paprika

1 kg (2 lb 4 oz) lamb fillet, trimmed and cut into 2 cm pieces

1 bay leaf

250 ml (9 fl oz/1 cup) vegetable stock

450 g (1 lb) baby potatoes, cut into 2 cm (¾ inch) pieces

100 g (3½ oz) fresh or frozen peas

3 tablespoons sour cream

sweet paprika, extra, to garnish

1 **Place the bacon** in a 4 litre (140 fl oz/16 cup) casserole dish and cook over medium heat for 4–5 minutes. Add the onion and cook for 2 minutes, then add the tomato and cook for 1 minute.

2 **Stir in the garlic**, caraway seeds, paprika, lamb, bay leaf and stock. Bring to the boil, then reduce the heat to low, and simmer, covered, for 40 minutes.

3 **Add the potato** and cook, uncovered, for 15 minutes, or until tender, then add the peas and cook for 5 minutes, or until tender. Stir in the sour cream and gently heat, without boiling. Garnish with paprika and serve with rye bread.

PORK AND WHITE BEAN CHILLI

SERVES 4

1.3 kg (3 lb) pork shoulder, boned, trimmed and cut into 2.5 cm (1 inch) cubes (700–800 g/1 lb 9 oz–1 lb 12 oz meat)

2–3 tablespoons oil

1 large onion, diced

3 cloves garlic, finely chopped

1 tablespoon sweet paprika

½ teaspoon chilli powder

2 tinned chipotle peppers or jalapeño chillies, chopped

1 tablespoon ground cumin

425 g (15 oz) can diced tomatoes

2 x 400 g (14 oz) cans cannellini beans, rinsed and drained

3 large handfuls coriander (cilantro) leaves, coarsely chopped

sour cream, to serve

lime wedges, to serve

1 Season pork. Heat 2 tablespoons oil in a large casserole dish over high heat. Add half the pork and cook for 5 minutes, or until brown. Remove. Repeat with the remaining pork, using more oil if necessary.

2 Lower the heat to medium, add the onion and garlic and cook for 3–5 minutes, or until soft. Add the paprika, chilli powder, chipotle peppers and cumin, and cook for 1 minute.

3 Return the pork to the pan. Add the tomato and 750 ml (26 fl oz/3 cups) water and simmer, partially covered, for 1–1½ hours, or until the pork is very tender. Add the beans and heat through. Boil a little longer to reduce the liquid if necessary. Stir in the coriander and season. Serve with sour cream and lime wedges.

SALSICCE WITH WHITE BEANS AND GREMOLATA

SERVES 4

3 tablespoons olive oil

12 salsicce or thick pork sausages, cut into chunks

6 garlic cloves, smashed

250 g (9 oz) chargrilled red or yellow capsicum (pepper)

2 x 400 g (14 oz) tins cannellini beans, rinsed and drained

1½ tablespoons grated lemon zest

6 tablespoons parsley, chopped

2 tablespoons lemon juice

extra virgin olive oil, for drizzling

1   Heat the olive oil in a frying pan and cook the salsicce until they are browned all over and cooked through. Lift them out of the frying pan with a slotted spoon and put them to one side.

2   Put 3 garlic cloves in the frying pan and cook them over a gentle heat until they are very soft. Cut the capsicum into strips and add them to the pan, along with the beans and salsicce. Stir together and cook over a gentle heat for 2 minutes to heat the salsicce through. Season well with salt and pepper.

3   To make the gremolata, smash the remaining 3 garlic cloves to a paste, with a little salt, in a mortar and pestle. Mix in the lemon zest and the chopped parsley and season with salt and pepper.

4   Just before serving, stir the gremolata through the beans and then finish the dish with the lemon juice and a drizzle of olive oil.

SATAY CHICKEN STIR-FRY

SERVES 4

1½ tablespoons oil

6 spring onions (scallions), cut into 2.5 cm (1 inch) lengths

800 g (1 lb 12 oz) skinless, boneless chicken breasts, thinly sliced on the diagonal

1–1½ tablespoons Thai red curry paste

4 tablespoons crunchy peanut butter

270 ml (9½ fl oz) coconut milk

2 teaspoons soft brown sugar

1½ tablespoons lime juice

jasmine rice, to serve

1 **Heat a wok** until very hot, add 1 teaspoon of the peanut oil and swirl to coat. When hot, add the spring onion and stir-fry for 30 seconds, or until softened slightly. Remove from the wok. Add a little extra peanut oil to the wok as needed and stir-fry the chicken in three batches for about 1 minute per batch, or until the meat just changes colour. Remove from the wok.

2 **Add a little more** oil to the wok, add the curry paste and stir-fry for 1 minute, or until fragrant. Add the peanut butter, coconut milk, sugar and 250 ml (9 fl oz/1 cup) water and stir well. Bring to the boil and boil for 3–4 minutes, or until thickened and the oil starts to separate—reduce the heat slightly if the sauce spits at you. Return the chicken and the spring onion to the wok, stir well and cook for 2 minutes, or until heated through. Stir in the lime juice and season. Serve with jasmine rice..

BUTTER CHICKEN

SERVES 4–6

2 tablespoons oil

1 kg (2 lb 4 oz) chicken thighs, quartered

60 g (2¼ oz) butter or ghee

2 teaspoons garam masala

2 teaspoons sweet paprika

2 teaspoons ground coriander

1 tablespoon finely chopped ginger

¼ teaspoon chilli powder

1 cinnamon stick

6 cardamom pods, bruised

350 g (12 oz) tomato passata (puréed tomatoes)

1 tablespoon sugar

3 tablespoons plain yoghurt

125 ml (4 fl oz/½ cup) pouring cream

1 tablespoon lemon juice

poppadoms, to serve

1 **Heat a wok** to very hot, add 1 tablespoon oil and swirl to coat the base and side. Add half the chicken and stir-fry for about 4 minutes, or until nicely browned. Remove from the wok. Add a little extra oil, if needed, and brown the remaining chicken. Remove from the wok and set aside.

2 **Reduce the heat** to medium, add the butter and stir until melted. Add the garam masala, paprika, coriander, ginger, chilli powder, cinnamon stick and cardamom pods, and stir-fry for 1 minute, or until the spices are fragrant. Return the chicken to the wok and mix in until coated in the spices.

3 **Add the puréed tomatoes** and sugar and simmer, stirring, for 15 minutes, or until the chicken is tender and the sauce is thick.

4 **Stir in the yoghurt**, cream and lemon juice and simmer for about 5 minutes, or until the sauce has thickened slightly. Serve with some poppadoms.

SAUSAGES AND MASH WITH SHALLOT GRAVY

SERVES 4

4 tablespoons olive oil

200 g (7 oz) French shallots, thinly sliced

1 tablespoon plain flour

125 ml (4 fl oz/½ cup) red wine

375 ml (13 fl oz/1½ cups) beef stock

1 tablespoon dijon mustard

1.5 kg (3 lb 5 oz) potatoes, chopped

150 g (5½ oz) butter

8 thick pork sausages
   (about 100 g/3½ oz each)

450 g (1 lb) green beans, topped and
   tailed

1 Heat 2 tablespoons oil in a large frying pan over medium heat. Add the French shallots and cook for 5 minutes, stirring often until they soften. Add the flour and cook for 30 seconds. Increase the heat, pour in the wine and stock and bring to the boil. Reduce the heat and simmer for 10 minutes, or until the gravy thickens. Stir in the mustard, then reduce the heat to medium–low and simmer gently until the sausages and mash are ready.

2 Cook the potatoes in boiling water until tender. Drain, return to the pan and add 1 tablespoon olive oil and 120 g (4 oz) butter. Mash until smooth, then season with salt and black pepper.

3 While the potatoes are cooking, prick the sausages with a fork. Heat a large frying pan over medium–high heat, add the remaining oil and the sausages. Cook for 10 minutes, or until cooked through, turning often.

4 Bring a saucepan of lightly salted water to the boil, add the beans and cook for 4 minutes, or until just tender. Whisk the remaining butter into the gravy and season. Place a mound of mash on each plate, top with the sausages and gravy, and serve with the beans on the side.

ROASTED VEAL CUTLETS WITH RED ONION

SERVES 4

1½ tablespoons olive oil

8 veal cutlets

4 garlic cloves, unpeeled

1 red onion, cut into thin wedges

1 tablespoon chopped rosemary

250 g (9 oz) cherry tomatoes

3 tablespoons balsamic vinegar

2 teaspoons soft brown sugar

2 tablespoons chopped flat-leaf (Italian) parsley

1 Preheat the oven to 200°C (400°F/Gas 6). Heat the oil in a large frying pan over medium heat. Cook the cutlets in batches for 4 minutes on both sides, or until brown.

2 Arrange the cutlets in a single layer in a large, shallow-sided roasting tin. Add the garlic, onion, rosemary, tomatoes, vinegar and sugar. Season well with salt and freshly ground black pepper.

3 Cover tightly with foil and roast for 15 minutes. Remove the foil and roast for another 10–15 minutes, depending on the thickness of the veal chops.

4 Transfer the cutlets, garlic, onion and tomatoes to serving plates. Stir the pan juices and spoon over the top. Garnish with the chopped parsley and serve immediately. Delicious with a creamy garlic mash and a tossed green salad.

BAKED CANNELLONI MILANESE

SERVES 4

500 g (1 lb 2 oz) minced (ground) pork and veal

50 g (2 oz/½ cup) dry breadcrumbs

2 eggs, beaten

1 teaspoon dried oregano

100 g (3½ oz/1 cup) grated parmesan cheese

12–15 instant cannelloni tubes

375 g (13 oz) fresh ricotta cheese

60 g (2¼ oz/½ cup) grated cheddar cheese

TOMATO SAUCE

425 ml (15 fl oz) tinned tomato passata (puréed tomatoes)

425 g (15 oz) tin crushed tomatoes

2 garlic cloves, crushed

3 tablespoons chopped basil

1 **Preheat the oven** to 180°C (350°F/Gas 4). Lightly grease a rectangular casserole dish.

2 **In a bowl**, combine the pork and veal, breadcrumbs, egg, oregano and half the parmesan cheese, and season to taste. Use a teaspoon to stuff the cannelloni tubes with the mixture. Set aside

3 **To make the tomato sauce**, bring the tomato passata, tomato and garlic to the boil in a saucepan. Reduce the heat and simmer for 15 minutes. Add the basil and pepper, to taste, and stir well.

4 **Spoon half the** tomato sauce over the base of the prepared dish. Arrange the stuffed cannelloni tubes on top. Cover with the remaining sauce. Spread with ricotta cheese, then sprinkle with the combined remaining parmesan and cheddar cheeses. Bake, covered with foil, for 1 hour. Uncover and bake for another 15 minutes, or until golden. Cut into squares to serve.

GNOCCHI WITH GORGONZOLA AND SAGE SAUCE

SERVES 4

2 x 500 g packets potato gnocchi

3 tablespoons butter

2 garlic cloves, crushed

10 g (¼ oz/½ cup) small sage leaves

100 g (3½ oz) gorgonzola cheese

150 ml (5 fl oz) cream

100 g (3½ oz/1 cup) grated parmesan
   cheese

1 **Preheat the grill (broiler)** to high. Lightly grease four 250 ml (9 fl oz/1 cup) heatproof gratin dishes. Cook the gnocchi in a large saucepan of rapidly boiling salted water according to the packet instructions until al dente. Lift the gnocchi out with a slotted spoon, leave to drain, then divide among the prepared dishes.

2 **Melt the butter** in a small saucepan over medium heat, add the garlic and sage leaves and cook for a few minutes, or until the leaves start to crispen and the garlic browns a little. Pour the sage butter evenly over the gnocchi in the gratin dishes.

3 **Dot small knobs** of the gorgonzola evenly among the gnocchi. Pour the cream over the top of each dish and sprinkle with the parmesan cheese. Place the dishes under the grill and cook until the top starts to brown and the gnocchi are heated through. Serve with a fresh green salad.

Note: This can also be cooked in a 1 litre (35 fl oz/4 cups) rectangular heatproof ceramic dish or round pie dish.

ITALIAN BEEF CASSEROLE WITH POLENTA DUMPLINGS

SERVES 4–6

2 tablespoons olive oil

1 onion, sliced

2 garlic cloves, crushed

1 tablespoon plain (all-purpose) flour

1 kg (2 lb 4 oz) blade or chuck steak, cut
   into 3 cm (1¼ inch) cubes

375 ml (13 fl oz/1½ cups) beef stock

1 tablespoon chopped fresh oregano

2 x 425 g (15 oz) cans tomatoes

2 red capsicums (peppers), roasted,
   peeled and cut into strips

100 g (3½ oz/⅔ cup) instant polenta

4 tablespoons ready-made pesto

1 **Preheat the oven** to 150°C (300°F/Gas 2). Heat the oil in a 4 litre (140 fl oz/16 cup) flameproof casserole dish, add the onion and garlic, and cook over medium heat for 8 minutes, or until soft but not brown. Sprinkle flour over the top and stir well. Add beef, stock, oregano, tomato and capsicum, season and simmer for 15 minutes, then bake, covered, for 1½ hours.

2 **Place 300 ml (10½ fl oz) water** in a saucepan, bring to the boil, then reduce the heat and simmer. Pour in the polenta in a thin stream, season and cook, stirring, for 2 minutes, or until it thickens and comes away from the side of the pan. Remove and cool.

3 **Shape the cooled** polenta into 12 round dumplings, place on top of the casserole and bake, covered for 1 hour, and then uncovered for a further 20–30 minutes. Garnish with the pesto and serve.

SERVES 4

850 g (1 lb 14 oz) veal shanks (osso buco)

2 tablespoons olive oil

1 large carrot, finely chopped

1 large onion, finely chopped

3 garlic cloves, crushed

250 ml (9 fl oz/1 cup) dry white wine

1 bay leaf, crumbled

800 g (1 lb 12 oz) tinned diced tomatoes

375 ml (13 fl oz/1½ cups) chicken stock

GREMOLATA

1 garlic clove, finely chopped

2 tablespoons finely chopped parsley

1 teaspoon finely grated lemon zest

1 anchovy fillet, rinsed and finely chopped

1 Preheat the oven to 150°C (300°F/Gas 2). Season the shanks. Heat the oil over medium heat in a flameproof casserole dish, add the shanks and brown on all sides. Remove. Add the carrot, onion and garlic, and cook for 3–5 minutes, or until softened. Stir in the wine and bay leaf, and cook for 5 minutes, or until reduced by half. Return the shanks, and add the tomato and stock. Bring to the boil. Cover, place in the oven and cook, turning the meat occasionally, for 1¾ hours–2 hours, or until the meat is tender.

2 Remove the shanks and cool slightly. Remove the meat from the bones and chop coarsely. Push the marrow out of the bones and discard the bones. Return the meat and marrow to the tomato sauce and cook on the stovetop for 20 minutes, or until reduced slightly. Season.

3 Combine the gremolata ingredients. Serve the osso buco with gremolata, and fettucine, if desired.

TUNA MORNAY

SERVES 4

4 tablespoons butter

2 tablespoons plain (all-purpose) flour

500 ml (17 fl oz/2 cups) milk

½ teaspoon dry mustard

90 g (3¼ oz/¾ cup) grated cheddar cheese

600 g (1 lb 5 oz) tinned tuna in brine, drained

2 tablespoons finely chopped parsley

2 eggs, hard-boiled and chopped

4 tablespoons fresh breadcrumbs

paprika, for dusting

1 Preheat the oven to 180°C (350°F/Gas 4). Melt the butter in a small saucepan, add the flour and stir over low heat for 1 minute. Take the pan off the heat and slowly pour in the milk, stirring with your other hand until you have a smooth sauce. Return the pan to the heat and stir constantly until the sauce boils and thickens. Reduce the heat and simmer for another 2 minutes. Remove pan from the heat, whisk in the mustard and two-thirds of the cheese—don't stop whisking until you have a smooth, rich cheesy sauce.

2 Roughly flake the tuna with a fork, then tip it into the cheesy sauce, along with the parsley and egg. Season with a little salt and pepper, then spoon the mixture into four 250 ml (9 fl oz/1 cup) ovenproof ramekins.

3 Make the topping by mixing together the breadcrumbs and the rest of the cheese, then sprinkle it over the mornay. Add a hint of colour by dusting the top very lightly with paprika. Place in the oven until the topping is golden brown, about 20 minutes.

SPICED BEEF AND ONION STEW

SERVES 4

1 kg (2 lb 4 oz) chuck steak, trimmed of excess fat and sinew
3 tablespoons olive oil
750 g (1 lb 10 oz) baby onions
3 garlic cloves, halved lengthways
125 ml (4 fl oz/½ cup) red wine
1 cinnamon stick
4 whole cloves
1 bay leaf
1 tablespoon red wine vinegar
2 tablespoons tomato paste (concentrated purée)
¼ teaspoon cracked black pepper
2 tablespoons currants

1 Cut the meat into bite-sized cubes. Heat the oil over medium heat in a large heavy-based saucepan. Add the onions and stir for 5 minutes, or until golden. Remove from the pan and drain on paper towels. Add the meat to the pan and stir over high heat for 10 minutes, or until the meat is well browned and almost all the liquid has been absorbed.

2 Add the garlic, wine, spices, bay leaf, vinegar, tomato paste, pepper, some salt and 375 ml (13 fl oz/1½ cups) water to the pan and bring to the boil. Reduce the heat, cover and simmer for 1 hour, stirring occasionally. Return onions to the saucepan, add the currants and stir gently. Simmer, covered, for 15 minutes. Discard the cinnamon before serving with rice or potatoes.

IRISH BEEF HOTPOT

SERVES 4

1 kg (2 lb 4 oz) chuck steak, cut into
 2.5 cm (1 inch) cubes

seasoned flour, to coat

2 tablespoons olive oil

2 large onions, sliced

2 garlic cloves, crushed

2 bay leaves

2 teaspoons chopped thyme

1 tablespoon chopped parsley

375 ml (13 fl oz/1½ cups) beef stock

4 potatoes, cut into 3 cm (1¼ inch)
 cubes

2 carrots, cut into 2 cm (¾ inch) pieces

1 Preheat the oven to 170°C (325°F/Gas 3). Toss the meat in the seasoned flour to coat. Heat the oil in a frying pan over medium heat, add the beef in batches and cook for 4–5 minutes, or until browned. Drain and place in a 4 litre (140 fl oz/16 cup) flameproof casserole dish.

2 Add the onion and garlic to the frying pan and cook for 5 minutes, or until softened and lightly golden. Add the bay leaves, thyme and half the parsley, stirring, then pour in the stock, stirring to remove any sediment stuck to the base or side of the pan. Transfer the stock mixture to the casserole dish, cover and bake for 1½ hours.

3 Add the potato and carrot to the casserole dish, and add a little water, if necessary. Return to the oven and cook for 1 hour, or until the meat and vegetables are tender. Garnish with the remaining parsley.

Note: This dish is delicious if made a day ahead and gently reheated.

BEEF STROGANOFF

SERVES 4

500 g (1 lb 2 oz) rump steak

2 tablespoons plain (all-purpose) flour

2 tablespoons olive oil

1 onion, finely chopped

1 garlic clove, crushed

400 g (14 oz) button mushrooms, sliced

1 tablespoon tomato paste
   (concentrated purée)

300 g (10½ oz) sour cream

finely chopped parsley, to serve

1 Trim the excess fat off the meat and slice it across the grain into thin pieces. Put the flour in a plastic bag and season well with salt and cracked black pepper. Add the steak and shake to coat the meat. Shake off any excess flour.

2 Heat 1 tablespoon oil in a large heavy-based frying pan over high heat. Add the meat and cook in batches until well browned. Remove from the pan and set aside.

3 Heat remaining oil and add the onion. Cook 2–3 minutes, or until soft and translucent, then add the garlic and stir briefly. Add the mushrooms and cook for about 3 minutes, or until soft. Stir in the tomato paste and sour cream, then add beef strips. Stir until well combined and heated through. Sprinkle with chopped parsley before serving with rice.

SPANISH-STYLE CHICKEN CASSEROLE

SERVES 4

2 tablespoons light olive oil

750 g (1 lb 10 oz) chicken thighs

750 g (1 lb 10 oz) chicken drumsticks

1 large onion, chopped

2 garlic cloves, crushed

2 teaspoons sweet paprika

1 large red capsicum (pepper), seeded
   and membrane removed, sliced

200 ml (7 fl oz) dry sherry

400 g (14 oz) tin peeled tomatoes

2 tablespoons tomato paste
   (concentrated purée)

165 g (6 oz/¾ cup) green olives, pitted,
   halved

1 teaspoon sweet paprika, extra

1 **Preheat the oven** to 180°C (350°F/Gas 4). Heat the oil in a large frying pan, add the chicken in batches and cook over medium heat for 3–4 minutes, or until browned. Transfer to a 4 litre (140 fl oz/16 cup) flameproof casserole dish. Add the onion, garlic, paprika and capsicum to the frying pan and cook for about 6 minutes, or until softened. Add sherry and cook for 2 minutes, or until slightly reduced. Add tomatoes and tomato paste, stir well and cook for 2 minutes. Pour tomato mixture over the chicken and add 250 ml (9 fl oz/1 cup) water.

2 **Bake, covered**, for 1¼ hours, then uncovered for a further 15 minutes. Add the olives and leave for 10 minutes. Garnish with the extra paprika and serve with rice.

BEEF MASALA WITH COCONUT RICE

1 tablespoon oil

1 kg (2 lb 4 oz) chuck steak, trimmed and cut into 2 cm (¾ inch) cubes

1 large onion, thinly sliced

3 garlic cloves, chopped

4 tablespoons ready-made tikka masala curry paste

2 teaspoons tamarind concentrate (from Asian supermarkets)

2 x 400 ml (14 oz) tins coconut milk

4 curry leaves

300 g (10½ oz/1½ cups) jasmine rice

1 Heat the oil in a large saucepan over high heat. Add the meat and cook in three batches for 4 minutes per batch, or until evenly browned.

2 Reduce heat to medium, add the onion to the pan, cook for 5 minutes, then add the garlic and cook for 1 minute. Stir in curry paste and tamarind for 30–60 seconds, until fragrant. Return the beef to the pan, add 550 ml (19 fl oz) coconut milk and the curry leaves and bring to the boil. Reduce the heat and simmer gently for 1½ hours, or until the meat is tender and the sauce has reduced. Add some water if the sauce starts to stick to the base of the pan.

3 Meanwhile, to make coconut rice, wash and thoroughly drain the rice. Put the rice, the remaining coconut milk and 250 ml (9 fl oz/1 cup) water in a saucepan and bring slowly to the boil, stirring constantly. Boil for 1 minute, then reduce the heat to low and cook, covered tightly, for 20 minutes. Remove from the heat and leave, covered, for 10 minutes. Fluff the rice with a fork before serving. To serve, season to taste and remove the curry leaves if you wish. Serve with the rice.

CYPRIOT PORK AND CORIANDER STEW

SERVES 4–6

1½ tablespoons coriander (cilantro) seeds

800 g (1 lb 12 oz) pork fillet, cut into 2 cm (¾ inch) cubes

1 tablespoon plain (all-purpose) flour

3 tablespoons olive oil

1 large onion, thinly sliced

375 ml (13 fl oz/1½ cups) red wine

250 ml (9 fl oz/1 cup) chicken stock

1 teaspoon sugar

coriander (cilantro) sprigs, to garnish

1 **Crush the coriander seeds** with a mortar and pestle. Combine the pork, crushed seeds and ½ teaspoon cracked pepper in a bowl. Cover and marinate overnight in the fridge.

2 **Combine the flour** and pork and toss. Heat 2 tablespoons oil in a frying pan and cook the pork in batches over high heat for 1–2 minutes, or until brown. Remove.

3 **Heat the remaining oil**, add the onion and cook over medium heat for 2–3 minutes, or until just golden. Return the meat to the pan, add the wine, stock and sugar, and season. Bring to the boil, then reduce the heat and simmer, covered, for 1 hour.

4 **Remove the meat.** Return the pan to the heat and boil over high heat for 3–5 minutes, or until reduced and slightly thickened. Pour over the meat and top with the coriander.

BEEF COOKED IN GUINNESS WITH CELERIAC PURÉE

SERVES 4

2 tablespoons oil

1 kg (2 lb 4 oz) chuck steak, cubed

2 onions, chopped

1 garlic clove, crushed

2 teaspoons soft brown sugar

2 teaspoons plain (all-purpose) flour

125 ml (4 fl oz/½ cup) Guinness

375 ml (13 fl oz/1½ cups) beef stock

1 bay leaf

2 sprigs thyme

1 celeriac

1 potato, cubed

250 ml (9 fl oz/1 cup) milk

1 tablespoon butter

4 slices baguette, toasted

1 teaspoon dijon mustard

1 Preheat the oven to 180°C (350°F/Gas 4). Heat half of the oil in a frying pan over high heat and fry the meat in batches until it is browned all over. Add more oil as you need it. Put the meat in a casserole dish.

2 Add the onion to the frying pan and fry it gently over low heat. When the onion starts to brown, add the garlic and brown sugar and cook until the onion is fairly brown. Stir in the flour, then transfer to the casserole dish.

3 Put the Guinness and stock in the frying pan and bring it to the boil, then pour into the casserole dish. Add the bay leaf and thyme to the casserole dish and season well. Bring to the boil, put a lid on and put the casserole in the oven for 2 hours.

4 Peel and chop the celeriac. Put the pieces into a bowl of water as you cut them. Put the potato and celeriac in a saucepan with the milk and bring to the boil. Cover and cook for 15 minutes, then mash everything together with the milk. Season well and add the butter.

5 Spread the bread with the mustard and serve with the beef ladled over and the celeriac purée on the side.

CHICKEN PIE WITH FETA

SERVES 6

1 kg (2 lb 4 oz) boneless, skinless
   chicken breast

500 ml (17 fl oz/2 cups) chicken stock

60 g (2¼ oz) butter

2 spring onions (scallions),
   finely chopped

75 g (2½ oz/½ cup) plain
   (all-purpose) flour

125 ml (4 fl oz/½ cup) milk

8 sheets filo pastry (30 x 40 cm/
   12 x 16 inch)

3 tablespoons butter, extra, melted

200 g (7 oz) feta, crumbled

1 tablespoon chopped dill

1 tablespoon snipped chives

¼ teaspoon freshly grated nutmeg

1 egg, lightly beaten

1 **Cut the chicken** into bite-sized pieces. Pour the stock into a saucepan and bring to the boil over high heat. Reduce the heat to low, add the chicken and poach gently for 10–15 minutes, or until chicken is cooked through. Drain, reserving the stock. Add enough water to the stock in order to bring the quantity up to 500 ml (17 fl oz/2 cups). Preheat the oven to 180°C (350°F/Gas 4).

2 **Melt the butter** in a saucepan over low heat, add the spring onion and cook, stirring, for 5 minutes. Add the flour and stir for 30 seconds. Remove the pan from the heat and gradually add the chicken stock and milk, stirring after each addition. Return to the heat and gently bring to the boil, stirring. Simmer for a few minutes, or until the sauce thickens. Remove from the heat.

3 **Line an ovenproof dish** measuring 4 x 18 x 25 cm (1½ x 7 x 10 inches) with four sheets of filo pastry, brushing one side of each sheet with extra melted butter as you go. Place the

pastry buttered side down. The filo will overlap the edges of the dish. Cover the unused filo with a damp tea towel (dish towel) to prevent it drying out.

4 **Stir the chicken**, feta, dill, chives, nutmeg and egg into the sauce. Season to taste. Pile the mixture on top of the filo pastry in the dish. Fold the overlapping filo over the filling and cover the top of the pie with the remaining four sheets of filo, brushing each sheet with melted butter as you go. Scrunch the edges of the filo so they fit in the dish. Brush the top with butter. Bake for 45–50 minutes, or until the pastry is golden brown and crisp.

Note: If you prefer, you can use puff pastry instead of filo pastry. If you do so, bake in a 220°C (425°F/Gas 7) oven for 15 minutes, then reduce the temperature to 180°C (350°F/Gas 4) and cook for another 30 minutes, or until the pastry is golden.

SERVES 6

FILLING

2 tablespoons oil

1 kg (2 lb 4 oz) trimmed chuck steak, cubed

1 large onion, chopped

1 large carrot, finely chopped

2 garlic cloves, crushed

250 ml (9 fl oz/1 cup) beef stock

2 tablespoons plain (all-purpose) flour

2 teaspoons thyme

1 tablespoon worcestershire sauce

PASTRY

250 g (9 oz/1⅔ cups) plain (all-purpose) flour

150 g (5½ oz) chilled butter, cubed

1 egg yolk

2–3 tablespoons iced water

1 egg yolk, to glaze

1 tablespoon milk, to glaze

1 Lightly grease a 23 cm (9 inch) pie dish. To make the filling, heat half of the oil in a frying pan and brown the meat in batches. Remove from the pan. Heat the remaining oil, add the onion, carrot and garlic and brown over medium heat.

2 Return the meat to the pan and stir in the flour. Cook for 1 minute, then remove from the heat and stir in the stock and flour. Add the thyme and worcestershire sauce and bring to the boil. Season to taste.

3 Reduce the heat, cover and simmer for 1½–2 hours, or until the meat is tender. During the last 15 minutes of cooking, remove the lid and allow the liquid to reduce so that the sauce is very thick and suitable for filling a pie. Cool.

4 To make the pastry, sift the flour into a bowl. Rub in the butter until it resembles fine breadcrumbs. Add the egg yolk and 2 tablespoons of the water and mix until the mixture comes together in beads. Turn out onto a floured work surface and gather together to form a smooth dough. Wrap in plastic wrap and refrigerate for 30 minutes.

5 Preheat the oven to 200°C (400°F/Gas 6). Divide the pastry in half and roll out one piece between two sheets of baking paper until large enough to line the pie dish. Line the dish with the pastry, fill with the cold filling and roll out the remaining pastry to cover the dish. Brush the pastry edges with water. Lay the pastry over the pie and press to seal. Trim any excess pastry. Re-roll the scraps to make shapes and press on the pie.

6 Cut steam holes in the top of the pastry. Beat together the egg yolk and milk and brush over the top of the pie. Bake for 20–30 minutes, or until golden.

SLOW-COOKED LAMB SHANKS

SERVES 4

2 tablespoons olive oil

8 French-trimmed lamb shanks

1 onion, chopped

2 garlic cloves, crushed

3 dried mace blades or 1½ teaspoons ground mace

2 teaspoons garam masala

500 ml (17 fl oz/2 cups) tomato pasta sauce

375 ml (13 fl oz/1½ cups) beef stock

1 tablespoon thyme

mashed potato, to serve

1 **Preheat the oven** to 150°C (300°F/Gas 2). Heat the oil in a large roasting tin or flameproof casserole dish and cook the lamb in batches for 5 minutes, or until browned all over. Remove from the tin and set aside. Add the onion and garlic to the tin and cook over medium heat for 3 minutes, or until soft. Stir in the mace and garam masala and cook for 30 seconds, or until fragrant.

2 **Return the lamb** to the tin with the pasta sauce and stock and bring to a boil. Cover tightly with a lid or foil.

3 **Roast in the oven**, covered, for about 4 hours, turning twice during cooking. Serve the lamb sprinkled with the thyme and accompanied by mashed potato.

BEEF AND RED WINE STEW

SERVES 4

1 kg (2 lb 4 oz) diced beef

3 tablespoons seasoned plain (all-purpose) flour

1 tablespoon oil

150 g (5½ oz) bacon, diced

8 bulb spring onions, greens trimmed to 2 cm (¾ inch)

200 g (7 oz) button mushrooms

500 ml (17 fl oz/2 cups) red wine

2 tablespoons tomato paste (concentrated purée)

500 ml (17 fl oz/2 cups) beef stock

1 bouquet garni

1 **Toss the beef** in the seasoned flour until evenly coated, shaking off any excess. Heat the oil in a large saucepan over high heat. Cook the beef in three batches for about 3 minutes, or until well browned all over, adding a little extra oil as needed. Remove from the pan.

2 **Add the bacon** to the pan and cook for 2 minutes, or until browned. Remove with a slotted spoon and add to the beef. Add the spring onions and mushrooms and cook for 5 minutes, or until the onions are browned. Remove.

3 **Slowly pour the red wine** into the pan, scraping up any sediment from the bottom with a wooden spoon. Stir in the tomato paste and stock. Add the bouquet garni and return the beef, bacon and any juices to the pan. Bring to the boil, then reduce the heat and simmer for 45 minutes, then return the spring onions and mushrooms to the pan. Cook for 1 hour, or until the meat is very tender and the sauce is glossy. Serve with steamed new potatoes or mash.

SPICY SEAFOOD GUMBO

SERVES 6

3 tablespoons olive oil

3 tablespoons plain (all-purpose) flour

1 large onion, chopped

2 celery stalks, chopped

1 red capsicum (pepper), seeded and
   membrane removed, chopped

2 bay leaves

3 garlic cloves, crushed

3 teaspoons finely chopped thyme

1½ teaspoons cayenne pepper

2 teaspoons sweet smoked paprika

3 teaspoons ground cumin

2 teaspoons ground oregano

1 litre (35 fl oz/4 cups) chicken stock

400 g (14 oz) tin chopped tomatoes

1 tablespoon tomato paste
   (concentrated purée)

350 g (12 oz) okra, ends trimmed,
   thickly sliced

1 kg (2 lb 4 oz) raw prawns (shrimp),
   peeled and deveined

300 g (10½ oz) large scallops, roe and
   muscle removed

400 g (14 oz) firm white fish fillets, cut
   into 4 cm (1½ inch) pieces

18 oysters, shucked

1 tablespoon chopped flat-leaf (Italian)
   parsley

worcestershire sauce, to taste

lemon wedges and rice, to serve

1 Put the oil and flour in a large saucepan over medium–low heat. Stir constantly for about 30 minutes, or until the colour of milk chocolate. Add the onion, celery, capsicum and bay leaves and cook for 15 minutes, or until the onion is softened. Increase the heat to high and add the garlic, thyme, cayenne, paprika, cumin and oregano. Cook for 1 minute, or until fragrant.

2 Stir in the chicken stock, 375 ml (13 fl oz/1½ cups) water, tomatoes and tomato paste and bring to the boil. Reduce to a simmer and cook for 1 hour. Add okra and cook for a further 45 minutes, or until okra is tender and sauce is thickened.

3 Increase the heat to high, add the prawns, scallops, and fish and cook for a further 5–6 minutes, then add the oysters. Cook for a further minute, or until all the seafood is just cooked through.

4 Stir through the parsley. Season with worcestershire sauce, salt and pepper. Serve with the rice and lemon wedges for squeezing over.

SPANISH SAFFRON CHICKEN AND RICE

SERVES 4

3 tablespoons olive oil

4 chicken thighs

6 chicken drumsticks

1 large red onion, finely chopped

1 large green capsicum (pepper), seeded and membrane removed, two-thirds diced and one-third sliced thinly

3 teaspoons sweet paprika

400 g (14 oz) tin diced tomatoes

275 g (10 oz/1¼ cups) paella or arborio rice

½ teaspoon ground saffron

1   Heat 2 tablespoons of the oil in a large deep frying pan over high heat. Season the chicken pieces well and brown in batches. Remove the chicken from the pan.

2   Reduce the pan to medium heat and add remaining oil. Add the onion and the diced capsicum and cook gently for 5 minutes. Stir in paprika and cook for 30 seconds. Add the tomato and simmer for 1–3 minutes, or until it thickens.

3   Stir 875 ml (30 fl oz/3½ cups) boiling water into the pan, then add the rice and saffron. Return the chicken to the pan and stir to combine. Season, to taste. Bring to the boil and cover. Reduce heat to medium–low and then simmer for 20–30 minutes, or until all the liquid has been absorbed and the chicken is tender. Stir in the thinly sliced capsicum, then allow to stand, covered, for 3–4 minutes before serving.

VEAL CASSEROLE WITH GREMOLATA

SERVES 4

3 tablespoons olive oil

1 large onion, chopped

1 celery stalk, chopped

2 teaspoons baharat, plus 1 tablespoon extra

3 garlic cloves, chopped

1 tablespoon plain (all-purpose) flour

4 large 5 cm (2 inch) thick pieces veal osso buco

30 g (1 oz) butter

125 ml (4 fl oz/½ cup) dry white wine

400 g (14 oz) tin chopped tomatoes

250 ml (9 fl oz/1 cup) chicken or beef stock

pasta, such as risoni, to serve

GREMOLATA

1 handful finely chopped parsley

2 garlic cloves, finely chopped

finely grated zest of 1 lemon

1 **Preheat the oven** to 160°C (315°F/Gas 2–3). Heat 1½ tablespoons of the oil in a heavy-based casserole dish. Cook the onion, celery and baharat for 3 minutes. Add the garlic and cook for a further 2 minutes, or until softened. Remove to a side dish.

2 **Combine the flour** and the extra baharat. Coat the cut sides of the meat in the flour mixture. Heat the remaining oil and the butter. Brown the veal on both sides over high heat. Arrange the veal in a single layer in the casserole dish. Add the white wine, bring to the boil and evaporate the wine by half.

3 **Mix together the** onion mixture and tomatoes and pour over the veal. Add the stock, or enough to just cover the meat. Cut a sheet of baking paper to fit over the meat. Cover with a lid. Bake for 1½ hours, or until the veal is very tender.

4 **To make the gremolata,** combine all the ingredients. Carefully remove the cooked meat from the casserole dish and boil the sauce for 5–10 minutes, or until reduced a little and syrupy. Spoon off any surface fat.

5 **To serve,** put the osso buco on serving plates, top with some sauce and sprinkle with gremolata. Serve with pasta.

COQ AU VIN

SERVES 4

1 tablespoon olive oil

12 white baby onions, peeled

3 rindless slices bacon, chopped

40 g (1½ oz) butter

1.5 kg (3 lb 5 oz) chicken pieces

2 garlic cloves, crushed

375 ml (13 fl oz/1½ cups) dry red wine

2 tablespoons brandy

1 tablespoon chopped thyme

1 bay leaf

4 parsley stalks

250 g (9 oz) button mushrooms, halved

1 tablespoon butter, extra, softened

1 tablespoon plain (all-purpose) flour

chopped parsley, to serve

1 Preheat the oven to 170°C (325°F/Gas 3). Heat the oil in a large heavy-based frying pan and add onions. Cook until browned, then add the bacon and cook until browned. Remove the bacon and onions and add the butter to the pan. When the butter is foaming add the chicken in a single layer and cook in batches until well browned. Transfer chicken to an ovenproof dish, draining it of any fat. Add onions and bacon.

2 Tip any excess fat out of the frying pan and add garlic, wine, brandy, thyme, bay leaf and parsley stalks. Bring to the boil and pour over the chicken. Cook, covered, in the oven for 1 hour 25 minutes, then add the mushrooms and cook for 30 minutes. Drain through a colander and reserve the liquid in a pan. Keep the chicken warm in the oven.

3 Mix the softened butter and flour together, bring the liquid in the pan to the boil and whisk in the flour and butter paste in two batches, then reduce the heat and simmer until the liquid thickens slightly. Remove the parsley stalks and bay leaf then return chicken to the ovenproof dish and pour in the sauce. Scatter on the chopped parsley and serve.

SWEET

NURSERY RICE PUDDING

SERVES 4–6

140 g (5 oz/⅔ cup) arborio or short-grain rice

1 litre (35 fl oz/4 cups) milk

4 tablespoons caster (superfine) sugar

1 teaspoon natural vanilla extract

125 ml (4 fl oz/½ cup) cream

1 **Rinse the rice** in a colander until the water runs clear. Drain well and place in a heavy-based pan with the milk, sugar and vanilla.

2 **Bring to the boil** while stirring, then reduce the heat to the lowest setting and cook for about 45 minutes, stirring frequently, until the rice is thick and creamy.

3 **Remove the pan** from the heat and leave to stand for 10 minutes. Stir in the cream. Serve warm.

Variations: Add a cinnamon stick and a strip of lemon zest to the rice in place of vanilla extract. Or add a small sprig of washed lavender to the rice while cooking.

BAKED RICE PUDDING

SERVES 4–6

melted butter, for greasing

3 tablespoons short-grain white rice

3 eggs

3 tablespoons caster (superfine) sugar

435 ml (15 fl oz/1¾ cups) milk

125 ml (4 fl oz/½ cup) pouring cream

1 teaspoon natural vanilla extract

¼ teaspoon nutmeg

1 **Preheat the oven** to 160°C (315°F/Gas 2–3) and brush a 1.5 litre (52 fl oz/6 cup) ovenproof dish with the melted butter.

2 **Cook the rice** in a large saucepan of boiling water for 12 minutes, or until tender, then drain well.

3 **Place the eggs** in a bowl and beat lightly. Add the sugar, milk, cream and natural vanilla extract, and whisk until well combined. Stir in the cooked rice, pour into the prepared dish and sprinkle with nutmeg.

4 **Place the dish** in a deep roasting tin and pour enough hot water into the tin to come halfway up the side of the dish.

5 **Bake for 45 minutes**, or until the custard is lightly set and a knife inserted into the centre comes out clean. Remove the pudding dish from the roasting tin and leave for 5 minutes before serving. Serve with poached or stewed fruit.

Variation: Add 2 tablespoons of sultanas (golden raisins) or chopped, dried apricots to the custard mixture before baking.

BREAD AND BUTTER PUDDING

SERVES 4

melted butter, for greasing

40 g (1½ oz) unsalted butter

8 thick slices day-old white bread

1 teaspoon ground cinnamon

2 tablespoons sultanas (golden raisins)

3 eggs

1 egg yolk

3 tablespoons caster (superfine) sugar

250 ml (9 fl oz/1 cup) milk

500 ml (17 fl oz/2 cups) pouring cream

½ teaspoon natural vanilla extract

1 tablespoon demerara sugar

1 Preheat the oven to 180°C (350°F/Gas 4). Brush a 1.5 litre (52 fl oz/6-cup) ovenproof dish with the melted butter

2 Spread the bread very lightly with the remaining butter and cut each slice in half diagonally. Layer the bread in the prepared dish, sprinkling the cinnamon and sultanas between each layer.

3 Lightly whisk together the eggs, egg yolk and caster sugar in a large bowl.

4 Heat the milk with the cream until just warm and stir in the vanilla extract.

5 Whisk the cream mixture into the egg mixture. Strain the custard over the layered bread, then leave for 5 minutes. Sprinkle with the demerara sugar.

6 Bake for 30 minutes, or until the custard has set and the bread is golden brown.

CHOCOLATE CROISSANT PUDDING

SERVES 6–8

melted butter, for greasing

4 croissants, torn into pieces

125 g (4½ oz) good-quality dark chocolate, chopped into pieces

4 eggs

5 tablespoons caster (superfine) sugar

250 ml (9 fl oz/1 cup) milk

250 ml (9 fl oz/1 cup) cream

3 teaspoons orange liqueur

3 teaspoons grated orange zest

4 tablespoons orange juice

2 tablespoons roughly chopped hazelnuts

whipped cream, to serve

1 Preheat the oven to 180°C (350°F/Gas 4). Brush the base and side of a 20 cm (8 in) deep-sided cake tin with the melted butter and line the bottom of the tin with baking paper. Put the croissant pieces into the tin, then scatter over 100 g (3½ oz) chocolate pieces.

2 Beat the eggs and sugar together until pale and creamy. Heat milk, cream and liqueur and remaining chocolate pieces in a saucepan until almost boiling. Stir to melt the chocolate, then remove the pan from the heat. Gradually add to the egg mixture, stirring constantly. Next, stir in the orange zest and juice. Slowly pour the mixture over the croissants, allowing the liquid to be fully absorbed before adding more.

3 Sprinkle the hazelnuts over the top. Bake for 50 minutes, or until a skewer comes out clean when inserted in the centre. Cool for 10 minutes. Turn the pudding out and invert onto a serving plate. Slice and serve warm with a dollop of cream.

CRÈME CARAMEL

SERVES 6

CARAMEL

100 g (3½ oz) caster (superfine) sugar

650 ml (22 fl oz) milk

1 vanilla bean

125 g (4½ oz) caster (superfine) sugar

3 eggs, beaten

3 egg yolks

1 **To make the caramel,** put the sugar in a heavy-based saucepan and heat until it dissolves and starts to caramelize—tip the saucepan from side to side as the sugar cooks to keep the colouring even. Remove from the heat and carefully add 2 tablespoons water to stop the cooking process. Pour into six 125 ml (4 fl oz/½ cup) ramekins and leave to cool.

2 **Preheat the oven** to 180°C (350°F/Gas 4). Put the milk and vanilla bean in a saucepan and bring just to the boil. Mix together the sugar, eggs and egg yolks. Strain the boiling milk over the egg mixture and stir well. Ladle into the ramekins and place in a roasting tin. Pour enough hot water into the tin to come halfway up the sides of the ramekins. Cook for 35–40 minutes, or until firm to the touch. Remove from the tin and leave for 15 minutes. Unmould onto plates and pour on any leftover caramel.

BAKED CUSTARD

SERVES 4

melted butter, for greasing

3 eggs

4 tablespoons caster (superfine) sugar

500 ml (17 fl oz/2 cups) milk

125 ml (4 fl oz/½ cup) cream

1½ teaspoons natural vanilla extract

nutmeg

1 Preheat the oven to 160°C (315°F/Gas 2–3). Brush four 250 ml (9 fl oz/1 cup) ramekins or a 1.5 litre (52 fl oz/6 cup) ovenproof dish with the melted butter.

2 Whisk together the eggs and sugar in a large bowl until they are combined.

3 Place the milk and cream in a small saucepan and stir over medium heat for 3–4 minutes, or until the mixture is warmed through, then stir into the egg mixture with the natural vanilla extract. Strain into the prepared dishes and sprinkle with the nutmeg.

4 Place the dishes in a deep roasting tin and add enough hot water to come halfway up the side of the dishes.

5 Bake for 25 minutes for the individual custards, or 30 minutes for the large custard, or until it is set and a knife inserted into the centre comes out clean.

6 Remove the custards from the roasting tin and leave for 10 minutes before serving.

Variation: Omit vanilla and add 1½ tablespoons Amaretto (almond-flavoured liqueur) or Grand Marnier (orange-flavoured liqueur) before baking.

APPLE CRUMBLE

SERVES 4

melted butter, for greasing

8 apples

4 tablespoons caster (superfine) sugar

zest of 1 lemon

125 g (4½ oz) butter

125 g (4½ oz/1 cup) plain (all-purpose) flour

1 teaspoon ground cinnamon

cream, to serve

1   **Preheat the oven** to 180°C (350°F/Gas 4). Brush a small baking dish with the melted butter. Peel and core the apples, then cut them into chunks. Put the apple, 2 tablespoons of the sugar and the lemon zest in the dish and mix them together. Dot 2 tablespoons of butter over the top.

2   **Rub the remaining** butter into the flour until you have a texture that resembles coarse breadcrumbs.

3   **Stir in the rest** of the sugar and the cinnamon. Add 1–2 tablespoons of water and stir the crumbs together so they form bigger clumps.

4   **Sprinkle the crumble** mixture over the apple and bake the crumble for 1¼ hours, by which time the top should be browned and the juice bubbling up through the crumble. Serve with cream.

SERVES 6

melted butter, for greasing

500 ml (17 fl oz/2 cups) milk

50 g (1¾ oz) unsalted butter

140 g (5 oz/1¾ cups) fresh breadcrumbs

115 g (4 oz/½ cup) caster (superfine) sugar, plus 1 tablespoon extra

finely grated zest of 1 orange

5 eggs, separated

210 g (7½ oz/⅔ cup) orange marmalade

1 teaspoon honey

whipped cream, to serve

1 **Preheat the oven** to 180°C (350°F/Gas 4). Lightly brush a 1.25 litre (44 fl oz/5 cup) rectangular ovenproof dish with the melted butter.

2 **Combine milk** and butter in a small saucepan and heat over low heat until the butter has melted. Put breadcrumbs, the extra sugar and orange zest in a large bowl. Stir in the milk mixture and set aside for 10 minutes.

3 **Lightly whisk the egg yolks**, then stir them into the breadcrumb mixture.

4 **Spoon the mixture into the** prepared dish, then bake for 25–30 minutes, or until firm to touch.

5 **Combine the marmalade** and honey in a saucepan and heat over low heat until melted. Pour evenly over the pudding.

6 **Whisk the egg whites** in a clean, dry bowl until stiff peaks form. Gradually add the sugar, whisking well, until the mixture is glossy and the sugar has dissolved.

7 **Spoon the meringue** evenly over the top of the pudding. Bake for 12–15 minutes, or until the meringue is golden. Serve the pudding warm with whipped cream.

RHUBARB AND BERRY CRUMBLE

SERVES 4

melted butter, for greasing

850 g (1 lb 14 oz) rhubarb, cut into 2.5 cm (1 inch) lengths

150 g (5½ oz/1¼ cups) blackberries

1 teaspoon grated orange zest

250 g (9 oz/1 cup) caster (superfine) sugar

125 g (4½ oz/1 cup) plain (all-purpose) flour

115 g (4 oz/1 cup) ground almonds

½ teaspoon ground ginger

150 g (5½ oz) chilled unsalted butter, cubed

thick (double/heavy) cream or ice cream, to serve

1   Preheat oven to 180°C (350°F/Gas 4). Lightly brush a deep 1.5 litre (52 fl oz/6 cup) ovenproof dish with melted butter.

2   Bring a saucepan of water to the boil over high heat, add rhubarb, and cook for 2 minutes, or until just tender. Drain well and combine with the berries, orange zest and 4 tablespoons of caster sugar. Taste and add a little more sugar, if needed. Spoon the fruit mixture into the prepared dish.

3   To make the topping, combine the flour, ground almonds, ginger and remaining sugar. Rub butter into the flour mixture with your fingertips until it resembles coarse breadcrumbs. Sprinkle the crumble mixture over the fruit, pressing lightly. Don't press too firmly, or it will become flat and dense.

4   Put the dish on a baking tray. Bake for 25–30 minutes, or until the topping is golden and the fruit is bubbling. Leave for 5 minutes. Serve warm with thick cream or ice cream.

APPLE SAGO PUDDING

SERVES 4

melted butter, for greasing

4 tablespoons caster (superfine) sugar

100 g (3½ oz/½ cup) sago

600 ml (21 fl oz) milk

55 g (2 oz/½ cup) sultanas
   (golden raisins)

¼ teaspoon salt

1 teaspoon natural vanilla extract

pinch nutmeg

¼ teaspoon ground cinnamon

2 eggs, lightly beaten

3 small ripe apples, peeled, cored and
   sliced

1 tablespoon soft brown sugar

thick cream or ice cream, to serve

1 Preheat the oven to 180°C (350°F/Gas 4). Lightly brush a 1.5 litre (52 fl oz/6-cup) ceramic soufflé dish with the melted butter.

2 Heat the sugar, sago, milk, sultanas and salt in a saucepan over medium heat, stirring often. Bring to the boil, then reduce the heat and simmer for 5 minutes.

3 Stir in the natural vanilla extract, nutmeg, cinnamon, eggs and the apple slices.

4 Pour into the prepared dish. Sprinkle with the brown sugar and bake for 45 minutes, or until set and golden brown. Serve warm with thick cream or ice cream, if desired.

STICKY DATE PUDDINGS

SERVES 6

melted butter, for greasing

180 g (6½ oz/1 cup) dates, pitted and roughly chopped

1 teaspoon bicarbonate of soda (baking soda)

75 g (2½ oz) unsalted butter, softened

155 g (5½ oz/⅔ cup) soft brown sugar

1 teaspoon natural vanilla extract

2 eggs

185 g (6½ oz/1¼ cups) self-raising flour, sifted

100 g (3½ oz/1 cup) walnut halves, roughly chopped

CARAMEL SAUCE

155 g (5½ oz/⅔ cup) soft brown sugar

60 g (2¼ oz) unsalted butter

250 ml (9 fl oz/1 cup) pouring cream

1 Preheat the oven to 180°C (350°F/Gas 4). Lightly brush six 250 ml (9 fl oz/1 cup) moulds with the melted butter and line the bases with circles of baking paper.

2 Put the dates and bicarbonate of soda in a saucepan and pour in 250 ml (9 fl oz/1 cup) water. Bring to the boil, remove from the heat and set aside to cool.

3 Beat the butter, sugar and vanilla with electric beaters until light and creamy. Add 1 egg, beat well and fold through 1 tablespoon of the flour. Add the other egg and repeat.

4 Fold through the remaining flour, walnuts and date mixture, and mix well.

5 Divide the mixture among the moulds, filling them three-quarters full. Bake for 30–35 minutes, or until slightly risen and firm to the touch.

6 To make the caramel sauce, put the brown sugar, butter and cream in a pan and simmer for 5 minutes.

7 Prick a few holes in each pudding using a skewer. Drizzle with some of the caramel sauce and return to the oven for about 5 minutes.

8 Loosen the side of each pudding with a small knife, turn out, remove the baking paper and serve with the remaining sauce.

CHOCOLATE PUDDINGS WITH RICH CHOCOLATE SAUCE

SERVES 6

melted butter, for greasing

1½ tablespoons unsweetened cocoa powder

120 g (4¼ oz) good-quality dark chocolate, chopped

120 g (4¼ oz) unsalted butter, softened

3 eggs, at room temperature

2 egg yolks, at room temperature

3 tablespoons caster (superfine) sugar

110 g (4 oz/¾ cup) plain (all-purpose) flour

CHOCOLATE SAUCE

80 g (3 oz/½ cup) chopped good-quality dark chocolate

125 ml (4 fl oz/½ cup) pouring cream

1 **Preheat the oven** to 180°C (350°F/Gas 4) and lightly brush six 125 ml (4 fl oz/½ cup) metal dariole moulds with the melted butter. Dust the moulds with the cocoa powder.

2 **Put the chocolate** in a small heatproof bowl over a small saucepan of simmering water, making sure the base of the bowl doesn't touch the water. Allow the chocolate to melt, then add the butter. When the butter has melted, stir to combine, then remove from the heat.

3 **Beat the eggs**, egg yolks and sugar in a large bowl using electric beaters until thick, creamy and pale in colour. Gently fold in the chocolate mixture. Sift in the flour and gently fold through.

4 **Spoon the mixture** into the prepared moulds, leaving about 1 cm (½ in) at the top of the moulds to allow the puddings to rise. Bake for 10 minutes, or until the top is firm and risen.

5 **Meanwhile**, to make the chocolate sauce, put the chocolate and cream in a heatproof bowl and melt over a small saucepan of simmering water, making sure the base of the bowl doesn't touch the water. Stir well.

6 **To serve**, run a knife around the moulds to loosen the puddings, then carefully turn out onto serving plates. Drizzle with the sauce and serve immediately.

BUTTERSCOTCH PUDDINGS

SERVES 4–6

melted butter, for greasing

150 g (5½ oz/1 cup) self-raising flour

4 tablespoons soft brown sugar

125 ml (4 fl oz/½ cup) milk

3 tablespoons butter, melted, cooled

1 egg

1 tablespoon golden syrup or honey

115 g (4 oz/½ cup) firmly packed soft brown sugar, extra

2 tablespoons golden syrup or honey, extra

1 **Preheat the oven** to 170°C (325°F/Gas 3). Lightly brush a 1.25 litre (44 fl oz/5-cup) ovenproof dish with the melted butter.

2 **Sift the flour** into a large bowl. Add the sugar.

3 **In a separate bowl**, whisk the milk, butter, egg and golden syrup together. Pour into the flour mixture and whisk until a smooth batter forms. Pour into the prepared dish. Place the dish on a baking tray.

4 **Sprinkle the extra** brown sugar over the batter. Combine the extra golden syrup and 310 ml (11 fl oz/1¼ cups) boiling water and carefully pour over the batter.

5 **Bake the pudding** for 35–45 minutes, or until a skewer inserted halfway into the pudding comes out clean.

6 **Set the pudding** aside for 5–10 minutes to allow the sauce to thicken slightly before serving.

PLUM COBBLER

SERVES 4

melted butter, for greasing

825 g (1 lb 13 oz) tinned dark plums, pitted

1 tablespoon honey

2 ripe pears, peeled, cored and cut into eighths

TOPPING

250 g (9 oz/1 cup) self-raising flour

1 tablespoon caster (superfine) sugar

¼ teaspoon ground cardamom or ground cinnamon

50 g (1½ oz) unsalted butter, chilled and chopped

3 tablespoons milk

extra milk, for brushing

1 tablespoon caster (superfine) sugar, extra

¼ teaspoon ground cardamom or ground cinnamon, extra

1 **Preheat the oven** to 200°C (400°F/Gas 6). Lightly brush an 18 cm (7 inch) round 1.5 litre (52 fl oz/6 cup) ovenproof dish.

2 **Drain the tinned plums**, reserving 185 ml (6 fl oz/¾ cup) of the syrup.

3 **Put syrup**, honey and pear in a large wide saucepan and bring to the boil. Reduce the heat and simmer for 8 minutes, or until the pear is tender. Add the plums.

4 **To make the topping**, sift the flour, sugar, cardamom and a pinch of salt into a large bowl. Rub in the butter with your fingers until it resembles fine breadcrumbs. Stir in the milk using a flat-bladed knife, mixing lightly to form a soft dough—add a little more milk, if needed.

5 **Turn onto a floured** surface and form into a smooth ball. Roll out to a 1 cm (½ inch) thickness and cut into rounds with a 4 cm (1½ inch) cutter.

6 **Spoon the hot fruit** into the dish, then arrange the circles of dough in an overlapping pattern over the fruit, on the inside edge of the dish only—leave the fruit in the centre exposed. Brush the dough with the extra milk. Mix the extra sugar and cardamom and sprinkle over the dough.

7 **Place the dish** on a baking tray and bake for 30 minutes, or until the topping is golden and cooked.

MIXED BERRY SPONGE PUDDINGS

SERVES 6

melted butter, for greasing

125 g (4½ oz) unsalted butter, softened

115 g (4 oz/½ cup) caster (superfine) sugar, plus 6 teaspoons extra

2 eggs

185 g (6½ oz/1⅓ cups) self-raising flour, sifted

3 tablespoons milk

200 g (7 oz) mixed berries, fresh or frozen

custard or ice cream, to serve

1 **Preheat the oven** to 180°C (350°F/Gas 4). Lightly grease six 125 ml (4 fl oz/½ cup) pudding or dariole moulds with the melted butter.

2 **Cream butter** and sugar in a bowl using electric beaters until pale and fluffy. Add eggs one at a time, beating well after each addition. Gently fold in the flour alternately with the milk.

3 **Divide the berries** between the moulds and top each with a teaspoon of the extra caster sugar. Top the berries with the pudding mixture, dividing the mixture evenly between the moulds.

4 **Put the puddings** in a large roasting tin and pour in enough hot water to come halfway up the sides of the moulds. Cover the baking tin with a sheet of baking paper, then cover with foil, pleating two sheets of foil together if necessary. Fold the foil tightly around the edges of the tin to seal.

5 **Bake puddings** for 35–40 minutes, or until the pudding springs back when lightly pressed. Remove the puddings from the water bath, leave to cool in the moulds for 5 minutes, then run a small knife around the inside of the mould and turn out onto plates. Serve with custard or ice cream.

LEMON DELICIOUS

SERVES 4–6

melted butter, for greasing

4 tablespoons unsalted butter, at room temperature

185 g (6½ oz/¾ cup) sugar

2 teaspoons finely grated lemon zest

3 eggs, separated

3 tablespoons self-raising flour

185 ml (6 fl oz/¾ cup) milk

4 tablespoons lemon juice

icing (confectioners') sugar, to dust

thick (double/heavy) cream, to serve

1 Preheat the oven to 180°C (350°F/Gas 4). Lightly brush a 1.25 litre (44 fl oz/5 cup) ovenproof ceramic dish with the melted butter.

2 Using an electric beater, beat the butter, sugar and grated zest together in a bowl until the mixture is light and creamy. Gradually add the egg yolks, beating well after each addition. Fold in the flour and milk alternately to make a smooth but runny batter. Stir in the lemon juice.

3 Whisk the egg whites in a dry bowl until firm peaks form and, with a large metal spoon, fold a third of the whites into the batter. Gently fold in the remaining egg whites, being careful not to overmix.

4 Pour batter into the prepared dish and place in a large roasting tin. Pour enough hot water into the tin to come one-third of the way up the side of the dish. Bake for 55 minutes, or until the top of the pudding is golden, risen and firm to the touch. Leave for 5 minutes before serving. Dust with icing sugar and serve with cream.

CARAMELIZED PINEAPPLE AND GINGER TARTE TATIN

SERVES 6–8

185 g (5¾ oz/1⅓ cups) plain
   (all-purpose) flour

1½ teaspoon ground ginger

85 g (3 oz) unsalted butter,
   cut into cubes

1 egg yolk

50 g (2 oz) glacé ginger, chopped

100 g (3½ oz) unsalted butter, extra

160 g (6 oz/¾ cup) caster (superfine)
   sugar

1 pineapple, peeled, quartered
   lengthways, cored and cut into
   5 mm (¼ inch) slices

thick (double/heavy) cream, to serve

1 **Put the flour**, ginger and butter in a food processor and process until the mixture resembles fine breadcrumbs. Add the egg yolk, glacé ginger and 2–3 tablespoons of water and pulse until the mixture comes together. Turn out onto a lightly floured surface and bring together in a ball. Cover with plastic wrap and place in the fridge for 20 minutes to rest.

2 **Melt the extra butter** in a 24 cm (9½ inch) ovenproof frying pan over low heat, add the sugar and stir until dissolved. Increase the heat to medium and cook, stirring, until the sugar starts to caramelize and turn golden brown (the mixture may go grainy then will go smooth). Reduce the heat to medium–low and add the pineapple slices. Cook for 15 minutes, or until the pineapple is tender and the caramel mixture is reduced and thickened slightly.

3 **Preheat the oven** to 180°C (350°F/Gas 4). Roll out the pastry between two sheets of baking paper to a disc slightly larger than the top of the frying pan. Lay the pastry over the top of the pineapple and tuck the edges down the side of the pan. Cook in the preheated oven for 35–40 minutes, or until the pastry is golden in colour.

4 **Carefully turn the tart** onto a large serving plate, cut into slices and serve with cream.

PEAR AND RASPBERRY CRUMBLE

SERVES 4

melted butter, for greasing

6 large pears (1.5 kg/3 lb 5 oz), ripe but firm

2 tablespoons caster (superfine) sugar

3 star anise

125 g (4½ oz/1 cup) raspberries

150 g (5 oz/1 cup) plain (all-purpose) flour

95 g (3¼ oz/½ cup) soft brown sugar

100 g (3½ oz) unsalted butter, cut into small cubes

ice cream, to serve

1 Preheat the oven to 190°C (375°F/Gas 5). Lightly brush a 1.5 Litre (52 fl oz/6 cup) ovenproof dish with melted butter

2 Peel, quarter and core the pears, then cut each piece in half lengthways. Put into a large saucepan, and sprinkle the sugar over. Add 1 tablespoon of water and the star anise. Cover and bring to the boil.

3 Cook, covered, over medium–low heat for 10 minutes, stirring occasionally, until the fruit is tender but still holds its shape. Drain the pears and discard the star anise, and transfer to the ovenproof dish. Sprinkle the raspberries over the pears.

4 Combine the flour, sugar and butter in a bowl. Use your fingertips to rub the butter into the flour until the mixture resembles coarse breadcrumbs. Sprinkle over the top of the fruit; bake for 20–25 minutes, until golden brown. Let stand for 5 minutes, then serve with ice cream.

INDEX

GREAT TASTES COMFORT FOOD

GREAT TASTES COMFORT FOOD